2026

Transhumanism
&
Contemporary Spirituality

Alexander J. Ziatyk

Transhumanism & Contemporary Spirituality

Alexander J. Ziatyk

2026

All rights are reserved. No part of this publication may be reproduced, stored in a retrieval system, or transmitted in any form or by any means, electronic, mechanical, photocopying, recording, or otherwise, without prior permission of the author. Enquiries concerning reproduction outside the scope of the above should be directed to the author.

FIRST EDITION

ISBN 979-8-9946607-0-6 Paperback

ISBN 979-8-9946607-1-3 E-book

The author has no responsibility for the persistence or accuracy of URLs for external or third-party Internet websites referred to in this publication and does not guarantee that any content on such websites is, or will remain, accurate or appropriate.

Contents

Introduction	7
The Seven Spheres and the Aberrant Eighth	19
Ahriman: The Lord of Darkness	33
Lucifer: The Lord of Light	39
The Task at Hand	45
Transmogrification: The Appearance of Paranormal Phenomena	66
The False Light	96
Climbing the Tree of Life	120
Developing Discernment	135
Interaction with Technology and the Stratification of Society	153
Precession of the Equinox	180
Balancing the Extremes	190
Putrefaction and Advent: The Rise, Fall and Rebirth of Institutions and Cults	201
The War on Consciousness	224

The Electronic Doppelgänger	242
Fearing Death is The Best Way to Ruin Your Life	256
The Only Way Out is Through	268
Bibliography	273

Introduction

You can feel it. Just under the surface, out of the corner of your eye, flitting by in the shadows, whispered in hushed voices, spoken of openly in only the most fringe of gatherings, a thought in the back of your mind, a gut reaction, an intuition barely registered – there is something strange occurring in our world unfolding at a pace which is breathtakingly rapid – too fast for most people to make sense of it. We sense it, but most of us dare not give voice to our concerns.

Technology has been foisted upon us over the last century like a tidal wave that could drown the world itself. Who asked for it? Did anyone vote for it? In 1968, when you, your parents or grandparents voted to elect the President of the United States, did you also vote for the silicon wafer microchip to be released onto the commercial market? Did you vote for it to be designed into all of our appliances and sold to us at a premium? No. You did not. No one did. Were you even aware it was happening? Yet what has had more of an impact on our civilization since that memorable year: the election of President Richard Nixon or the flooding of our civil infrastructure and personal spaces with the silicon wafer microchip?

It should be quite clear by now to anyone

with a head on their shoulders and a heart in their chest that politics, culture, social well-being and personal health have taken a back seat to the machinations of a handful of secretive technological sorcerers with delusions of grandeur and plans to disrupt and usurp the fundamental power dynamics of humanity. There are people who believe themselves worthy of the throne of the world, to reshape the world in their image, simply because they have a few technical insights into the material sciences, and they intend to use these material sciences as their sceptre of power.

Before you start calling me a conspiracy theorist, make sure you understand what the word "theory" means. What is theoretical about the fact that the microchip in your computer, in your phone, in your television, in your car, in your toaster oven for Pete's sake, was put there without your consent. That is a fact – not a theory. You are not allowed or able to participate in society unless you make religious and regular use of these microchips. That is a fact – not a theory.

Get rid of every appliance, every device, every thing whatsoever that has a microchip in it and attempt to make money. Try to have a proper working career that pays you enough money to pay your bills. Try paying your bills! Try feeding yourself. Attempt to have a vibrant social life with proper and fair sexual selection. Keep in mind, when attempting to do these things, you must not use anything with a microchip in it, either directly or indirectly.

Barring life in a highly populated thriving intentionally off-grid community with its own insular government, you will fail utterly in this task. You will starve, you will be poor, you will lose your home, the government will imprison you for tax evasion, you will be celibate, you will have little to no social access, in short, you will be exiled and set adrift.

I can hear the echo of a two thousand year old voice saying something about a mark... something about a beast... something about buying and selling... something about worshiping its image...

Maybe I'm just crazy. Only paranoid Christians say things like this, right?

The fact remains: our technological output has outpaced our ability to reason about technology – to get to grips with it, to decide whether or not we even want it or need it. We run the risk of outsourcing our own thinking, feeling and willing to machines. When this occurs, we become the thralls and slaves of the people who create and program these machines. They become a class of tyrants.

We will explore these prison-like

circumstances in this book. You will see that I am not encouraging anyone to become a Luddite. We will discover and endeavor to understand ways in which we can alter how we approach our technology and foster a more balanced and sacred interaction with it in an attempt to redeem the technology and our relationship with it.

***

And even beyond this more obvious phenomenon of the rapid and unlooked-for overhauling of our civilization is the feeling of an intense anti-spiritual impulse arising from beneath the deep reaches of our world. It infects the hearts and minds of millions and attacks the very foundations of our humanity, our traditions, our ancestry, our roots, our memory, our lived experience, our intuition, our depth of feeling, our cosmic connection, our connection to each other, our connection to the Divine, our fundamental knowing, our childish sense of wonder, our sense of place, and our coherent vision of a shared destiny. It is all under threat by something or someone. But what? Who? Is it a force of nature? An organic churning and changing of historical times? A trendy materialist philosophy from the Age of Enlightenment? An inorganic conspiracy of madmen? An arch demon from the chaotic realm of the Abyss? An imaginal phantasm given life by our collective urge toward hedonism and death? Is it really happening at all or am I imagining it?

Just under the surface of conventional life, if one squints hard enough, a grotesque shadow can be seen lurking and haunting the dark places. A cosmic horror that deceives and tricks at best and torments and destroys at worst. A force that defies conventional phenomenology stirs just beyond our sight; occasionally showing itself in the most bizarre and inexplicable phantasmagoria. There seems to be something supernatural or paranormal at work here. But that can't be true... can it?

Few dare plumb these depths for fear of going mad or discovering something that they worry ought not be discovered. Restful sleep will be replaced with restless pondering and desperate ontological terror. No wonder most people do not bother with such thinking and nervously laugh at or utterly shun those who do. Perhaps it is best to leave well-enough alone, to not rock the boat, and tattoo "ignorance is bliss" on the inside of one's eyelids and put one's head firmly back in the sand than attempt to answer such a fundamental and necessary question: Why is this age so damn dark?

But before you can ask this question, you must first realize and admit that we do indeed live in a dark age. The Greeks call it the Iron Age. The Vedics call it Kali Yuga. The Christians call it the Eschaton, or the End Times. But it seems many, if not most, people are so enamored and proud of this age and its technology as to believe we are progressing. They have been hypnotized by the religion of progress and fundamentally believe that the world and humanity get better as time moves forward. They do not question this. They do not even know that they can question it. They take this thought for granted and refuse to think other thoughts. Some know that there are thoughts which they are not permitted to think. Most do not even think that there are thoughts which they are not permitted to think. They know deep within their hearts that if they question the status quo, they will risk losing all of their social status, sexual selection, financial stability, political access, and their so-called "sanity."

When one is honest with oneself and realizes the state of the world, one immediately becomes pariah and can quickly feel alone in an ocean of human automata. These human automata can even be openly hostile toward an honest person. Who wants that? Best to be dishonest with oneself. It is a great deal easier and much more lucrative.

But know this: if you have felt this way and have seen the world as it is, you are not alone. There are many like you. Many more than you may realize. Most keep their heads down and keep silent with their opinions. Opening one's mouth is a dangerous game. But I have noticed when my courage peaks and I speak aloud my inner thoughts, like the slave-rebels on the hill with Spartacus, suddenly a dozen or more stand out of a crowd and declare, "I also feel this way. Thank you for speaking aloud that which I have been thinking and feeling."

***

This book was written to explore the fundamental phenomenology of technology and how humans interact with it. That may sound a bit dull like something Jacques Ellul or Norbert Wiener would write about in the 1950's, or pedantic like something you would find in a university book store, or perhaps reactionary like something a bearded bomb-maker might rant about before attempting to murder a computer scientist. As much as I have attempted to avoid these unfortunate angles, it is indeed possible that my book is all of these things at once, but it will also take into account the endlessly interesting and always surprising topics of parapsychology, spirituality and The Tradition.

It is my opinion that the discipline (as unpalatable to some as it may be) of parapsychology is of utmost importance when considering how a human being interacts with the world around them – especially in regards to modern technology. If you have delved into the work of the brilliant George P. Hansen or are familiar with the studies that were once carried out in places like the Rhine Research Center in North Carolina or the Psychophysical Laboratories in New Jersey, you will feel right at home with this topic. When we broach the subject in this book, we will be examining it less in its clinical setting and more in its application toward understanding paranormal phenomena and cognitive changes caused by ruptures in normal consciousness.

Parapsychology is one of the key foundational disciplines for recognizing and attempting to understand paranormal phenomena and human consciousness in general. I have found that it works as a great pallet-cleanser when one gets too caught up in researching through the lenses of either positivist scientific materialism or spiritual mysticism. It bridges the gap between the subject and the object and clears out cognitive cobwebs as it forces the researcher to think in ways that are easily left undiscovered by overly subjective inner-searching and overly objective outer-searching. And as an added bonus, if you study it enough, you will learn how to win at dice games without cheating.

I would like to acknowledge and recommend with a great deal of gratitude the works and studies of John Keel, Jacques Vallée and F.W. Holiday. I have been reading their books since childhood. Without the original and vibrant perspectives of these individuals, the light bulb of my mind would likely have remained a dim flicker and I would potentially have been lost in dogma the way many scientists, spiritualists, and paranormal researchers find themselves stuck in intellectual ruts fueled by stubbornness for the entirety of their lives. The interdisciplinarian approach of these authors, while perhaps not as rigorous as it could be, is extraordinarily profitable. They are unafraid to blend the fields of psychology, parapsychology, journalism, social science, computer science, history, material science, spiritual tradition, folklore and mythology and synthesize them with personal experience and anecdotal evidence. The value of their insights and data collection cannot be overstated.

***

Those of you who are familiar with the works of Julius Evola and René Guénon or have simply practiced a truly effective spiritual discipline for many years may already be familiar with The Tradition. It is essentially a human's birthright – the capability and imperative to connect to and fully engage with the fundamental reality and experience that fundamental reality in the fullest, absolute and most free capacity.

That sounds simple enough, right? Thankfully it is. However, it goes largely unrecognized in today's world due to certain types of interference that prevent clarity of thought, ease of perception, and openness of feeling. This interference is the main subject of this book. We will face down this interference toe-to-toe and stare it in its red glowing eyes. We will attempt to understand this obstacle so that we may equip ourselves with the tools necessary for spiritual awakening despite the chaos and darkness of the world around us.

This obstacle, or interference, is a strange and nebulous thing. Many people throughout the ages have attempted to name it, to tame it, to control it, to worship it, to protect themselves from it, to merge with it or to leave their mark upon it. An occult philosopher from the previous century named Rudolf Steiner called it the Eighth Sphere. A journalist and paranormal researcher who stumbled upon this phenomenon independently by the name of John Keel has dubbed it the Eighth Tower – a realm within his so-called Superspectrum. It is interesting to note the spontaneous similarity in terminology here regarding the number eight. Even the great fantasy author J.R.R. Tolkien intuited this eighth realm while synthesizing Celtic and Nordic folklore when he wrote his *Silmarillion*. He wrote about the seven light-filled creator gods who live and work in a beautiful harmony with each other and the eighth evil and dissonant deity known as Melkor who disrupts and perverts the great symphony of the world. It is like a perfect seven-note musical scale that seems to only be harassed by the introduction of an eighth note which sounds sour and out of tune with the rest.

It is interesting to ponder this musical analogy and take it to its conclusion. Some of the most beautiful works of music deliberately use what are known as "accidental notes" or "borrowed chords" from another musical scale that are not included in the seven-note root scale of the song that under normal circumstances would sound horrible, but under the guidance of a master composer, create something new, surprising and utterly beautiful. Keep this in mind when contemplating the contents of this book. While the Eighth Sphere may be a terrifying place, it is also part of the Symphony of the Cosmos.

***

Understanding the Eighth Sphere, the deceptive activities and manifestations of paranormal phenomena, the influx of modern digital, electrical and material technologies, and the anti-spiritual cultural and ideological currents taking hold around the world is all part of a crucial step in being a balanced and advanced spiritual human in this current era. It may seem that these topics are disparate and unrelated, but I will endeavor to show you that they are quite interrelated. And in seeing the interrelation amongst them, a pattern will be perceived which will automatically develop within the reader a higher perspective and a greater discernment. It is my wish that I will clear away much of the confusion and despair that many feel today and provide a personal way forward for each individual who confronts these difficulties and ideas in modern life.

The Seven Spheres and the Aberrant Eighth

What is the Eighth Sphere? What are the other Seven Spheres? Just what in the world is a Sphere anyway?

A sphere, from one perspective, is a world at a particular stage of its development. According to occultists like Rudolf Steiner[1] and G.I. Gurdjieff[2], organic processes occur in seven stages. Whether we are examining the life cycle of a human being, the life cycle of a tree, the way emotions arise and cease, the development and collapse of a civilization, or the existence through time of an entire planet, for the sake of observation, these cycles can all be divided into seven stages.

In the Vedic tradition, this development of a world is known as Anandatandava, or the Dance of Shiva, the cosmic interplay of creation and destruction. When Brahma, the Creator, falls asleep, he dreams the worlds into material existence. When Brahma awakens from this dream, the worlds disappear and are reabsorbed into the spiritual world, or the Godhead. When a world exists physically, this period of time is called a Manvantara. When the world is reabsorbed into spirit and ceases to materially exist, this period of time is called a Pralaya. This manifesting and reabsorbing occurs repeatedly like inhalation and exhalation.

From the Rosicrucian viewpoint described by Rudolf Steiner, each Manvantara and Pralaya brings with it a development for the world and its inhabitants[3]. During the earliest stage of a world's existence, in its first Manvantara, the planet can hardly be called a planet. It is in a nearly immaterial state, being still physically under-developed. Essentially, it is like a ball of warmth floating in space, and the humans who inhabit the world would not be recognized as we know them today. They, like the planet, would also appear like small globules of warmth and would be essentially invisible to normal eyesight. They would not have physical bodies made of minerals or water like ours are today. They would also lack certain spiritual and subtle bodies which we have today and would only possess "I" consciousness, a kind of spiritual ego of self-awareness. What we know as the soul, the ether body, and the physical body would not yet be developed.

After some time, perhaps millions of years, this world is reabsorbed into the spiritual world and the Pralaya begins. During this period, perhaps lasting an equal amount of time, the world is prepared for its next material manifestation by highly advanced spiritual entities. When it is birthed back into the material cosmos, it will now be composed of warmth and air. An atmospheric component will have been added to it. Also, the warmth element will now be within the humans who inhabit the world, and their bodies will also contain a new airy feature. They will also have developed an astral body, or the animal soul. A new material component is added to the world and to the human body, and a new spiritual component is added to the human being.

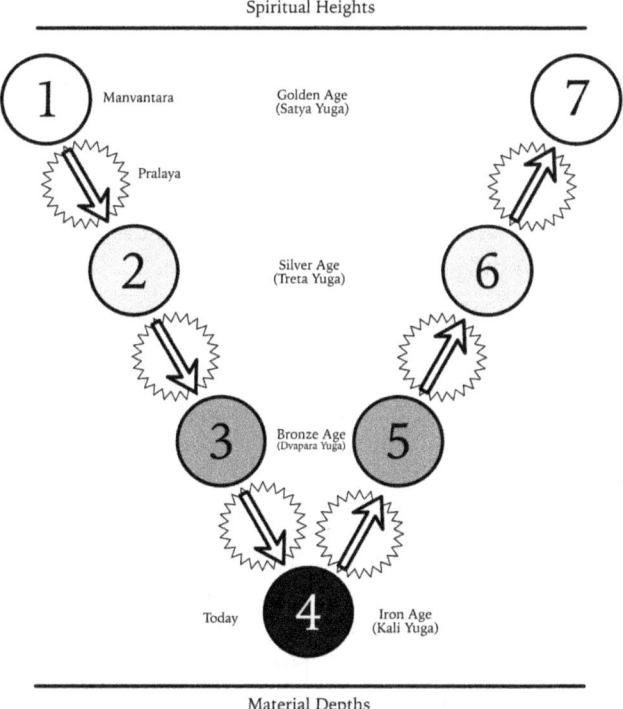

Another Pralaya occurs followed by another Manvantara.

In this Manvantara, the planet is even more materialized and will have descended one step "further" away from the spiritual world, or one step more densely into the world of matter. This time, a watery component will be added to the world and to the human body. A human being will now contain within itself warmth and air, and its body will be mostly composed of liquid. With this comes the development of the etheric body, or the subtle body of a human being that regulates health and metabolism and allows a connection between matter and spirit as the chakra system is now partially developed. We can see that the material components of the previous Manvantara become the inner world of a human during the next Manvantara.

Another Pralaya occurs followed by a new Manvantara.

Now we arrive at the current, or fourth, Manvantara in which we live in our present day where the mineral component is added to the world and the human body. The liquid, air, and warmth components of the previous Manvantaras are now part of a human being's inner world in the forms of emotions, thoughts, and will, respectively. The world is now very physical. Things are very solid and distinct. Our bodies are flesh, blood and bone. Everything around us has solid boundaries and is clearly discreet and separate from every other thing. We can step on the ground and bump our knees on the coffee table. We can high-five each other. There is hardly any nebulousness or mixing of things, except in the chemical and elemental combinations of molecules and alloys. The world is at its lowest, heaviest, and most material stage that it will ever experience.

The development up to this point has been described as The Fall according to Christian tradition. Buddhist tradition considers it the descent into Maya, or illusion. The ancient Rishis considered it a type of forgetting, falling asleep and entering a dream state called Samsara. The Greeks consider it the descent into an Iron Age of madness and confusion, far flung from the earliest Golden Age[4]. The Vedics call it Kali Yuga, a far cry from the earliest, spiritual age of Satya Yuga[5]. It is the state at which we are the most ignorant of spiritual reality, when our perceptions can hardly detect spiritual phenomena and we become enamored of the material world. But on the bright side, it is also when humans begin to develop their most acute mental capabilities and their capacity for truly selfless behavior. I will explain that in this book as well.

From this point forward, according to the Rosicrucian and occult evolutionist conception, the next Manvantaras will be more spiritual. No more material components will be added to the world. Only spiritual features will now develop and the material features will be spiritualized. Our world has begun its ascent back toward a higher state thanks to a great turning point that occurred roughly two thousand years ago. The world experienced a great Messianic mystery at its lowest material descent and was provided with a spiritual resuscitation which has allowed humanity and the world to engage with the spiritual world in greater capacity.

All in all, there will be seven Manvantaras which will result in the complete spiritual and material development of human beings and the world. According to hints left by great prophets and seers from many traditions, humans have some kind of spiritual destiny related to the ending of the seventh Manvantara where we become part of the cosmic hierarchy and move on to greater creativity and usefulness. It's all very vague and mysterious and glorious and whatnot.

If there are seven Manvantaras, or Spheres, that exist according to the Divine plan, then when and where does this Eighth Sphere fit in?

While our world is here in its lowest, most material stage, it runs the risk of being derailed from its proper developmental path and permanently trapped in the material realm. It is a dangerous position to be in when a world has sunk this low. We are currently skating atop the very outer surface of the lower worlds, the hell worlds. Seers and prophets have warned that this can become a permanent condition if we fail in our spiritual tasks today. This pseudo-Manvantara of ultimate and permanent materiality that may be created can be called the Eighth Sphere.

This pseudo-Manvantara, this Eighth Sphere, will almost certainly be created whether we like it or not. It may already exist *in potentia* according to the Vedic cosmology of the fourteen Lokas, or worlds. There are seven spiritual heavenly worlds called Vyahrtis and seven lower hell worlds called Patalas. The Earth, or Bhur, is the lowest of the upper worlds, coming in at world number seven, and just beneath it is the eighth world called Atala, the highest of the hell worlds ruled by an asura, or dark deity, named Bala. While our world is in its densest, most material state, we are skating just above this realm. But this does not have to derail our world.

The Eighth Sphere will be created from our world, as matter and energy are drawn away from the Earth and used to build it (similarly to the stories about how our Moon was created by material from the Earth. This similarity explains why certain 19th and 20th century occultists confused the Moon with the Eighth Sphere.) But so long as a critical mass of humanity spiritualize their thinking and activity, the world itself will continue on its proper course and the Eighth Sphere will be left to exist on its own, like dropping dead weight. Christians may be hearing something in their minds about the separation of wheat and chaff. Well here it is. Some people will be lost to the Eighth Sphere. People are always lost by the time a Pralaya comes around. Those people who did not achieve their spiritual initiation, who did not meet the grade or make the cut during a Manvantara, do not graduate to the next Manvantara. They are "held back" so to speak and become the ghosts, demons, elementals, false gods and poltergeists of the next Manvantara.

The ones who do recognize the spiritual task set before them and meet this great challenge with a Herculean spiritual effort will indeed graduate and become a more advanced human during the next Manvantara. The ones who have been held back may attempt to latch onto the more advanced humans in an attempt to vicariously redeem themselves, or "hitch a ride into heaven" so to speak. Others who have been left behind may be full of hatred and resentment and may harass humanity in other ways. Some of these beings who prefer it, will find a new home within the Eighth Sphere and will choose to remain there once it has been fully established. There they will find and manufacture the virtual fantasies in which they may lose themselves in an attempt to fulfill their hedonism and delusion. Many of them, like the devil on the left shoulder whispering into the ear, are currently tempting vast numbers of human beings to fall with them into the Eighth Sphere by enticing them with the delights, distractions and conveniences that are part and parcel of modern digital technologies.

***

I have found an interesting correlation between this cosmological chronology and the more classical cyclical chronology of the Greeks, Taoists[6], Vedics and Traditionalists[7]. The Descent of the Ages was and still is a commonly held belief among many peoples, and it is quite different from the modern view of linear time and the belief in progress.

It is said that when the world was first created, it existed in a Golden Age of spirituality, truth, perfect justice, and perfect knowledge. The Vedics call it Satya (or Krita) Yuga. The Greeks believed that this age was ruled by the great titan Chronos. It was a time when the world was closest to the Tao. The Egyptians knew it as Zep Tepi, or "The First Time," when the gods walked among men. People did not age. They behaved like perfect ladies and gentlemen. There was no sickness, misery or toil. All was butterflies and rainbows.

But then Pandora just had to open Zeus'

jar. Eve just had to go apple picking. People just had to become witty and hypocritical. Some strife and conflict arose and the Golden Age descended into a Silver Age also known as Treta Yuga. The Greeks believed that Zeus ruled this era. People began to refuse to worship the gods, and to compensate for this, they focused on virtue instead of Tao. They lived much shorter lifespans and they quarreled with each other. After some time, the world slipped downward again.

The world lost more of its harmony. In this Bronze Age, also known as Dvapara Yuga, warfare became a pastime – violence, a way of life. Weapons manufacturing became a lucrative business and civil relations fell out of order. To alleviate this further degeneration away from Tao and unable even to practice virtue, people focused on family relations and paternal kindness. Humanism began to take hold in the minds and hearts of people. This age came to its conclusion with the Great Flood referenced in many traditions around the world.

Following this, there was a very brief and glorious age of heroes who recognized this descent and fought to improve the lot of humanity. But their efforts would be largely forgotten and only referenced in places such as *The Ramayana*, *The Iliad*, Celtic, Nordic and Slavic folklore and in some scant accounts within *The Old Testament*.

Finally, we come to the final age of this cycle – The Iron Age or Kali Yuga. According to the Greek and Vedic traditions, during this age, all honor is thrown out the window. People are miserable. They toil their lives away for money. Corruption, thievery, deception, betrayal and selfishness are commonplace and ignorance reigns supreme. People feel no guilt or shame, and in fact, they consider their selfish behavior to be virtuous and profitable. Family members fight and compete with one another. Liars are believed to be good and truth tellers are considered evil and inconvenient. The authentic spiritual traditions are replaced with empty ceremony. All social contracts are trampled underfoot. Guests are treated with suspicion and disdain. Seeking power for oneself is considered the highest good. The gods have utterly forsaken humanity and there is no hope against the rule of evil.

Sound familiar?

One need only look around at our civilization and our culture to realize that this description is quite accurate and becomes more true by the day. It is so obvious that I see little profit in pointing out the myriad facts which would prove this. It is sufficient to simply reflect for a moment.

This description seems to me like the

fourth Manvantara which is the most densely material Sphere explained in the Rosicrucian conception. In fact, it stands to reason that the Descent of the Ages and the Anandatandava are essentially portraying the same chronology and cosmology.

It is said that a great Avatar, an incarnation of God Himself, named Kalki, or was it Maitreya? Meshiach? The Second Coming? Anyway, someone is apparently due to arrive soon and save us from ourselves. Then all will be made right with the world. The whole thing will blow up and restart at a Golden Age and there shall be no more suffering. The New Agers have a similar belief in their Great Awakening. Even the atheists and materialists believe in some kind of Technological Singularity or a coming Machine God Messiah who will right all wrongs and end all woes real soon. Trust me! It's totally gonna happen, like, in a few days!

(Personally, I don't hold out hope for such prophecies. It seems like a mental illness to await someone to solve your problems for you if you are perfectly capable of taking steps to solve them yourself.)

There is a difference here at the end between this classical chronology and the modern Rosicrucian one. In the Rosicrucian scheme, the dark age does not end cataclysmically and reset straight back to a

Golden Age. Instead, it begins a gradual climb back up toward a Golden Age, toward the spiritual world, toward Tao. (I call it the sin wave theory of cycles, as opposed to the sawtooth wave theory.) This view was also held by Sri Yukteswar Giri and his student Paramhansa Yogananda, two yogis from India who lived in the 19th and 20th centuries and made it their mission to teach Westerners about traditional yoga and Eastern spiritual practice. They taught that the world was leaving Kali Yuga and entering into Dvapara Yuga on a gradual ascent toward Satya Yuga, and that there would be no great cataclysm[8]. At least not yet. This is in agreement with the modern occult view, but not with institutionalized "traditional" views. Use your own discernment when analyzing history.

***

I know that most of what I have said so far originates from the tradition of "revelation" or revealed dogma, meaning that someone said something or wrote something down about reality, and here it is! Cue the victory horns! You now know the mysteries of reality! Believe me, I know how awful it is to listen to some hackneyed idea that has been passed down from sophist to sophist. I went to university, too.

I am drawing from ancient religious texts, mythological cosmogonies, and modern clairvoyant occultists. I understand how distasteful this is to some.

      We know that there is also the tradition of "reason" which encourages discovery of facts using one's own consciousness[9]. I prefer this path and I imagine you do as well. I certainly do not expect you to simply believe everything I am telling you here. I know this revealed cosmology is quite strange and almost completely defies modern scientific logic. However, whether you consider it to be metaphorically true, factually true, or only vaguely symbolic, it will help you understand the events occurring in our world regarding changes in technology, culture, mentality and law. It will also help you understand parallel, hidden worlds and the irruption of paranormal phenomena in our world. If you stick with it, you will discover the path of reason, even if you only accept this cosmology as an analogy, and will not depend on this revelation.

Ahriman: The Lord of Darkness

If there is an aberrant world, an Eighth Sphere, being created as an alternative to the organic, natural and spiritual Spheres, then there must be someone or something behind it, a will, a driving force that enacts these designs. Indeed, there very well may be. Rudolf Steiner discovered this entity during his clairvoyant researches. When he met this being, he said that he felt heavy and slow and stuck as though he were trying to move through set concrete. Even I have felt the presence of something living, something with intelligence, something filled with envy and hatred guiding certain corporations, certain politicians, certain trends in culture, certain institutions, certain developments in technology, certain ways of thinking. A palpable spite can be felt emanating from certain personalities. An almost tangible hatred toward all things spiritual. And it is the same spite, the same venom, emanating from each different person as though there is a living spirit using some people as puppets. The similarities in mentality, word-choice, agenda, and feelings toward people and nature are easily recognizable and make one wonder if all of these people went to the same school, belong to the same secret society, or are being orchestrated by the same spiritual impulse. Perhaps it is a little of each, but when one catches a whiff of a conspiracy, one must search deeper beneath the surface and not become content with blaming certain people or groups. Although certainly there are people who must be held accountable for their actions, the buck does not necessarily stop with worldly and physical human beings. It can be deduced that there are deeper and darker non-human powers at work in these situations. Simply getting rid of the conspirators would not get rid of the problem. Treating the symptoms of a disease is not the same as curing it.

This spiritual impulse can be given a name, a personage. The ancient Persian Zoroastrians knew him as Ahriman (a.k.a. Angra-Manyu). Rudolf Steiner and many modern occultists and researchers have adopted this name due to its accuracy and aptness. When a Christian refers to Satan, they are generally referring to Ahriman. He is a spirit who governs much of material existence. He is bound to matter and is forbidden from entering the spiritual world. He desperately wishes to be free of this condition. He has the most influence over the force of electricity in which he expresses himself most effectively. Occultists know electricity by another name: Fallen Light. It is a materialized, almost non-spiritual version of spiritual power. It is almost like an inverted or opposite form of spiritual light. It is dangerous and wild, volatile and deadly and very difficult to harness properly. But it can and must be harnessed in order for humanity to utilize certain types of technology and fully benefit from materiality. One can think of Archangel Michael/St. George and the Serpent. He dominates the serpent in order to harness its power.

The human body also utilizes electricity for its autonomic functions to work. The central nervous system is governed by this power. When a human being is born in this Manvantara, Ahriman immediately enters into the newborn infant's body in the form of electricity and begins regulating its physical organs. Do not be afraid. This is not demonic possession. It is simply part of human life. It is best not to think of Ahriman as our enemy, but simply as an angry governor who wishes to rebel against the King and needs to be reminded of his place.

When the human being later dies and the material components of the body are reabsorbed by the Earth, the electricity also dissipates and is recycled into the material world. Meanwhile, the spiritual components of the human being re-enter the spiritual world. Ahriman is deeply disappointed by this. He wishes to latch onto the human's spiritual components and breach the gates of Heaven. Like the devil in John Milton's *Paradise Lost*, Ahriman wishes to develop machinery and techniques that he may use to latch onto or even replace the soul of a human and besiege and tear down the Pearly Gates to enter into the world of the Spirit.

Of course, such a feat is almost certainly impossible. It could only happen if God allowed it. However, in the attempt to achieve this goal, Ahriman will wreak havoc in the hearts, minds, and bodies of humanity and the sanctity of the Earth. In failing this goal, Ahriman will attempt to achieve his secondary objective. If he cannot enter Heaven, he would rather rule in Hell. He will reign over a world of his own creation, a world which he is designing to be free of the "tyranny" of God, a world over which he will have ultimate influence and control. This is the motivation behind his building of the Eighth Sphere. He is attempting to build a world of utter materialism and delusion so that there will be no spiritual access to it, so that no angel may enter in and disturb the hearts of his slaves and subjects, so that no influence from the Higher Powers may threaten his sovereignty.

Basically, he is a teenager who wants to put a lock on his bedroom door to try and keep his parents out because he wants to smoke weed and play videogames all day.

And indeed, many poor souls will be seduced and join him in this false world where there will be much weeping and gnashing of teeth. Those who are taken in by the promises of modern technology and the dogmas of science and give their personal sovereignty and power away to these gadgets, techniques and beliefs will find themselves cut off from the spirit and dependent on externalities for happiness and fulfillment. Since they will not draw upon the spirit for inner happiness and freedom, they will require constant entertainment, constant stimulation, constant financial increases, constant gene therapy and physical "improvements," constant pharmacopoeia, constant reassurance that they have chosen and are living a good life; they will be utterly dependent on technologies and external enjoyments because they will have an emptiness in their heart so large and vacuous that it will greedily devour anything that draws too close. We can see people developing along these lines today. They are prime candidates for citizenship within the Eighth Sphere.

During this Manvantara, our world has drawn heavily upon the realm of Ahriman. It was necessary for the material development of our world and our human bodies. But it is precarious. We are dancing with the devil. Never before have we been so close to the Lord of Darkness. Never have we felt his presence so strongly and surely. If Ahriman has his way, the entire world would be transformed into a giant electrical device. Nothing organic would remain. Vigilance and balance are more important today than they have ever been. If we can keep Ahriman in his place, dominate and subdue him and utilize his talents and aspects in a healthy way and from a position of spiritual strength, the human race will harness and benefit from immeasurable power.

Lucifer: The Lord of Light

Ahriman is not working alone in building the Eight Sphere. He is collaborating with another entity. This entity is often conflated and confused with either Ahriman or Satan. There is a commonly held misconception that Lucifer and Satan are the same entity; that he was named Lucifer while in Heaven, and after he was kicked out, he had his name legally changed on his driver's license to Satan. There is actually no biblical evidence or historical precedent for this belief aside from a handful of medieval and modern scribes and poets who felt a creative need to mix and merge together the characters of Lucifer, Satan and the Serpent in the Garden in order to etiologically explain the origin of witchcraft or to show off some fancy translation and etymology skills. Some scholars prefer to use the term Satan as a title for anything that is against God and nature due to the fact that it means "adversary" in the Hebraic tongue. They will label many different beings and forces as "Satan," and this can be a confusing generalization although technically accurate. It is the opinion of clairvoyant researchers such as Rudolf Steiner and C.G. Harrison that Lucifer, Ahriman and Satan are in fact different entities and the entity who has most fully earned the title Satan is currently referred to as Sorat (a.k.a. The Anti-Christ or the Demon of the Sun) in occult circles.

Perhaps I am splitting hairs, but it is important to understand the cosmic balancing act occurring here: the dark and the light, yin and yang, ossification and inflammation, cold and hot, matter and spirit, and so on. If Ahriman represents the extremism of materialism, then Lucifer represents the extremism of spiritualism. If they are both conflated with Satan, then the picture becomes unclear and discernment becomes difficult. There are two realms blending with each other in order the create the Eighth Sphere: the realm of matter and the realm of spirit. An overly ossified version of the material world is combining with the delusional and fantastical elements of the spiritual world. This combination creates a world of illusion and chaos that can serve as a prison for wayward souls.

In a similar way in which Ahriman is attempting to leave his material domain and enter the spiritual domain – a world which he has no right to be in – so too is Lucifer attempting to leave the spiritual world and enter into the material – a realm which he has no permission to access. Ahriman's goal is twofold: to either enter into the spiritual world and be free of his material condition, or failing that, to rule his own material world so as to have a sense of ultimate sovereignty over his own realm. Lucifer also has a twofold goal: to enter into the material world to experience all of its pleasures and enjoyments, since he is utterly spiritual, he cannot enjoy the sensory experiences offered by material incarnation. But should he fail in this endeavor, he seeks to destroy the world utterly, so that there is no material world. There will only exist the world of spirit and nothing will remain of which he is envious or desirous, or which causes suffering and ugliness, and he can have peace of mind. When people beg for nuclear war or believe that the world would be better off without humans or desire a sudden and complete cessation of suffering at the expense of all things, this is a Luciferic impulse.

Ahriman and Lucifer are attempting to enter into each other's realms and have influence there. This commingling of powers results in the creation of the Eighth Sphere, where both Lucifer and Ahriman can, to an extent, fulfill their desires. It also causes disruption within the human sphere. Human souls, minds, and bodies are influenced by the spiritual powers, including those of Ahriman and Lucifer. Some humans who lack self-awareness and spiritual discipline may be played like fiddles by the spiritual powers. With even a cursory observation, one can see the world-hating, world-denying aspects of many religious and New Age movements and political personalities that have a sympathy with the Luciferic impulse – whether the believers and participants realize it or not. And one can readily see the spirit-denying and materialistically-obsessed aspects of modern science, positivism, and certain political movements which have an unbalanced focus on economy, technology, identity, body, race or military.

***

The same analogy I used to describe Ahriman before also applies to Lucifer. He is not our enemy, he is merely a discontented governor seeking to rebel against his King.

These two great spirits must be kept in balance, kept in their respective places where they operate in healthy and normal ways. When Ahriman is kept in his place, the human body functions well and human beings have a healthy interest in the physical world around them and a desire to create new and innovative technologies for the sake of improving our experiences in this world. Remember Archangel Michael/St. George and the Serpent. Harness the power of the dragon. And when Lucifer is kept in his place, he provides us with our artistic and aesthetic impulses and inspires us to create great works of beauty and reach for our spiritual heights. Yearning for and moving toward the spirit is essential, and the Light Bearer is like a fishing lure that attracts us to do so. Just try not to bite the hook and get yanked out of this world too quickly. A human being should strive for a full and balanced development and not attempt to re-enter the spiritual world prematurely, or to deny the material world out of fear, hatred, or desperate avoidance of suffering, as the unbalanced Luciferic impulse would have us do.

That which keeps these two in balance is the Solar Logos, what some may refer to as the Christ Impulse - although it goes by many names. That Messianic spirit that exists within the hearts of all humans must be recognized, fostered and developed so that it may well up and shine forth from each and every one of us. In this way, clarity is achieved and doubt is removed regarding our society and technology and we are intuitively guided to make healthy choices regarding the phenomenal world and the spiritual world.

The Solar Logos holds these two spirits at bay and in chains, allowing them to move, operate, and govern only in the limited capacities which are proper and beneficial for themselves and the world. But human beings must make the choice based in free will to align their hearts and minds with this Divine Impulse, otherwise it may have no efficacy in this world. God will not override our free will. If you wish to plug your mind into the Matrix and enter the Eighth Sphere, you are free to do so. It must be a conscious choice and effort on your part to find and walk the Middle Way.

Do not get stuck on the nomenclature of the Solar Logos. There are many names, titles and concepts that identify this spiritual impulse: Christ, Krishna, Rama, Esus, Messiah, Meshiach, Maitreya, Mithras, Ahura Mazda/Ormuzd, Osiris/Horus, Vishnu, Kalki, Tammuz, Baldr/Odin, The Higher Self, The Prototypical Human, The Son, The Sixth Sphere of the Kaballah, The Logos, and so on. From the point of view of The Tradition, these names, titles and concepts are all synonymous and interchangeable.

The Task at Hand

Earlier I mentioned that, according to occult tradition, there are particular spiritual initiations which human beings must successfully face and achieve during each Manvantara in order to develop their being completely, organically, and properly. Each Manvantara will provide certain conditions for the human race to experience and encourage, or even force, them to develop certain spiritual faculties through difficult training and trials which are known as an initiation. It is never quite clear what the initiation is or how to achieve it during a given age. There is no instruction manual for this kind of thing. However, it can be surely identified by a simple method which does not require clairvoyance or any sort of psychic or spiritual gift. In this day and age, it only requires a few moments of quiet reflection. If you wish to identify the tasks you must perform and the behavior you must exhibit in order to develop more advanced spiritual faculties and freedoms, simply ask yourself this question: What is the most difficult thing for me and/or most people to do?

Whatever your answer is, there is your task.

Of course, I am asking for your discernment here. I am not asking you to find a ten thousand pound boulder and attempt to lift it, or to find the world's greatest technical problem and attempt to solve it. The answer should be something of which you are fully capable in your day-to-day life given the faculties which you currently possess. This task should be something you can do regularly and repeatedly and in most circumstances around most people.

A very common answer that I hear often is usually something along the lines of: "meditate more." I would argue that this is a step in the right direction but not good enough. Sure, you may find meditation challenging; it may be difficult to sit still, to quiet your mind, or to face yourself, but is it truly difficult? Do you really believe that sitting still and breathing is an initiation ritual or trial? You will have to think just a bit more deeply than that.

Meditation is extremely important and I highly recommend the regular practice of it. It will improve every aspect of your life and act as a support for your actual initiation, as it develops self-awareness and self-control. But meditation is just that – a support. It is not the goal. When your stomach is empty, you fill it with nutritious food. When your body is dirty, you bathe. When your body is weak, you strengthen it with exercise. Likewise, when your mind and spirit are out of order, you reconfigure and recharge yourself with meditation. It is part of hygiene and daily life; it is not your spiritual initiation. The choirs of angels do not sing in triumph because you ate when you were hungry. The heavens do not open up and pour forth their blessings upon you because you showered when you were dirty. An initiation is a great and dedicated effort, not a yoga retreat at Mount Shasta.

***

It is my opinion that the particular tasks of initiation with which we are all collectively faced in this particular stage of human development is to perform selfless actions and to control and transmute our emotions. These, I believe, are the most difficult things for most people to do for various reasons which I will now explain.

***

First, we will discuss selfless action.

Long, long ago, most people had an atavistic and primitive sense of clairvoyance. They could quite literally see into the spiritual world as though in a waking dream. The spirits, the deities, the invisible currents of the world were all part of daily life and an accepted part of reality. Our histories, religious texts, mythologies, folklore, cave paintings and epic poetry reveal this to be almost certainly true. Everyday life was very dream-like back in the day.

However lovely this might sound and however much Neo-Pagans and New Agers love to glorify and romanticize this period of human history, lamenting the loss of this clairvoyance, complaining about our modern state, and attempting to regain this wishy-washy dreamy vision, it is important to note that it was indeed atavistic; meaning, childish, undeveloped and outmoded. With it came a near-complete lack of freedom and free will on the part of humanity. In Homer's epic account which functioned as one of the principle religious texts of the Greek world, Achilles wanted to slay Agamemnon in the throne room, and Agamemnon pleaded for his life, arguing the finer points of virtue. Achilles' hand was not staid by love or compassion, his heart was not moved to forbearance; he fully intended to behead that king. It was Athena herself appearing from the supra-sensible world and grabbing Achilles' wrist which stopped the sword from swinging and spilling blood.

This was the common lot of humanity during the remote past. The gods essentially used us as puppets and playthings, and we had little choice in the matter. Who would dare stand against the obvious and visible might and terror of the gods aside from the bravest and stupidest Bronze Age heroes? Who could have the power to resist such frightful presences, forces and personages?

Another force which was visible and obvious to humanity during this age was the law of karma. To them, it was as apparent as gravity is to us. When we drop a stone, we know it will fall to the ground and we can see and understand how fast it will fall and how hard it will hit. There is no questioning or debating this point. It is an experiential fact. So too, was the law of karma at a certain point in human history. It is why the ancient Rishis were so familiar with these laws and were all in agreement about them.

When a person carried out a benevolent action, they would see how it affected the supra-sensible world and allowed benevolence to be returned to them in due course. When they performed a misdeed, they could readily observe, feel and understand the consequences of their actions and how it would be returned upon themselves.

This essentially renders selflessness impossible. How can a person truly act selflessly if they know for a fact that they will be rewarded for it? If a person can witness the law of karma the way we witness the law of gravity, their motivations for doing something benevolent or avoiding something malevolent may be entirely selfish due to the fact that they are aware of an incoming spiritual or material reward or punishment.

This is a horrible problem with karma

yogis in this day and age who are obsessed with balancing their own karmic checkbooks. They appear to be selfless, but they are merely desperate to be rewarded and terrified of being punished due to their dogmatic faith in and fear of the law of karma or the so-called "wrath of God" despite the fact that they cannot see this law playing out like we once did. This type of karma yoga is the hallmark of most institutionalized and exoteric forms of religion. We hear it in the confession booth, we feel it when the collection plate gets passed around, we see it in the Tarot reading room, we smell it on those who pay the sin eaters and trance channelers, we taste it on the bread and wine, and we hear it in the chanting of mantras and recitation of prayers. The fear, the desire, the desperation, the uncertainty of the future all welling up within a population who senses a Great Something just beyond their reach that may be either pleased or disappointed with their actions and possesses the unbridled and irresistible power to show both favor and vengeance in awful measure.

This fear and desire is a hangover from an earlier time. It is deeply entrained in our spiritual memory. The law of karma needed and needs to be forgotten. The fear of punishment and desire for reward need to be eliminated. This is why our clairvoyant faculties have been removed and we have been sunk into an almost entirely material world. We must learn to perform selfless actions not because we wish to be rewarded or avoid punishment from some cosmic judicial system, but because it is the right and proper thing to do. It is the correct way to have a healthy civilization and a beneficent life for all.

Follow the Golden Rule. Treat others the way you would like to be treated. Accomplish this task regularly and you will succeed in your initiation.

However, I am not asking you to be a pushover or to have misplaced compassion or to put yourself at risk in order to be nice to people or to go out of your way to offer help to people who neither want it, need it, deserve it, nor asked for it. There is a difference between being good and being nice. You must have strength and discernment. Good people know when to draw a line in the sand and set healthy boundaries. Nice people get stabbed in the spleen by thieves. You must stand up for yourself and plant your feet and resist and suppress monsters and criminals. Simply resist and suppress evil with serenity and unemotional justice, not anger or vengeance or hatred. Plant your feet with determination and Godly will, not with jealousy or pride. Take care of your needs and provide love and freedom for yourself with balance and good will, not with the modern toxic "self-help" and "self-care" which are thinly disguised narcissism and selfishness. I know that you possess this discernment and I have full faith that you will, or already have, achieved this balance.

At first, following the Golden Rule is quite difficult. When someone needs and deserves money, you give them money, but perhaps you are reluctant. Now you have less money. It came at a cost to you and you are not sure whether you will be rewarded. As far as you know, this was bad for you and good for the recipient of your money. You may feel slightly anxious now that your financial resources are diminished. You may also feel slightly warm and happy having done a good deed. You will have these mixed and confusing emotions.

This goes for a great variety of selfless activity. Your friend is moving and needs help hauling their junk from place to place. This is physically taxing, it is an enormous demand of your time, you will be paying for fuel in your car and lunches on the road, you may receive minor injuries, you may need an extra day to rest and recover, and at the end of it, all you get is a "Thanks, man. I appreciate it." A hint of resentment may well up within you for a time. Forgive yourself this feeling. It is only natural. Over time, you will stop resenting people who ask for your help and you will discern who is deserving of it and who is not. This discernment is a discipline that must be practiced.

But of course you will help your friend! He is your friend, after all. Is this not what friends are for, as they say? If he truly is your friend, you will not request or require a reward. You will know that you have improved his life, you have made him feel that much more secure and confident that his relationships are meaningful and beneficial, you will have inspired him to perform selfless actions for someone else (hopefully, if he is indeed a good person) which will improve the lives of others, and this cycle expands and increases like a field of flowers blooming in the sunlight, or like a single-cell organism exponentially multiplying itself and growing and thriving.

You will not be rewarded. At least you are not aware that you may be rewarded. The way it appears to you is that you have rewarded someone else at a personal cost to yourself. You have done this because you know it was the right thing to do; because you do not abandon those who are in need and who have reached out to you for help. Is this not what true royalty does? The King or the Queen is the one who hands out rewards. They are not rewarded. A proper Monarch in a healthy, normal and traditional civilization is like a servant to God and the people and a bridge between the Spirit and the World. They act as those who carry out sentences and offer rewards according to Divine Will. This is the center from which we must all act now. We must understand the royalty that flows within our souls and illuminates the world around us as it exudes from our being, having its origin in The Most High. Otherwise we will prove ourselves utterly unworthy of paticipating in any form of politics or government.

It gets easier and easier the more you do it. Selflessness and discernment are like muscles that need regular exercise. Surely we may hurt ourselves from time to time due to inexperience, lapse of judgment, or attempting to lift too much weight, but pain is an excellent teacher. Pain becomes wisdom, and wisdom becomes thoughtful actions which avoid pain and bring benefit to all. Regularity and perseverance are essential in this practice. It must become a lifestyle choice, and even more, it must become like breathing; natural, healthy, easy and effortless but with the discernment to breathe in clean air and avoid pollution and toxicity.

So the next time you lament your lack of clairvoyance or psychic sensitivities, next time you wish to curse this limited and puerile material world and the prison-like conditions it forces upon us, remember this: these conditions offer you a wonderful opportunity to practice a great challenge, to undergo a great Herculean effort to grow and develop your being in strength, grandeur, power and beauty, to become Kingly and Queenly, to expand your spirit and increase your capabilities by facing this difficult and fiery trial. You are metal in a forge, a lump of coal under pressure. Your efforts are enormous even though they seem tiny and small in your little daily choices: to be gentle in your power, to be generous in your poverty, to be selfless in your home, to be thoughtful in your work, to be compassionate in your hustle and bustle, to be full in your emptiness, to be temperate in your thoughts, to be self-controlled in your emotions, and to be modest in your beauty. A million tiny actions result in one unfathomably large soul experience. A journey is nothing more than many small steps in a vast sequence of steps. You do not need to move the Earth, you merely need to move a few hearts, even if at first it is just your own.

***

Next, we will discuss the transmutation and control of emotions as the second task of initiation in this era.

The Age of Pisces was and is an Age of emotionality and belief. (We will learn more about the Zodiacal Ages in the chapter entitled The Precession of the Equinox.) Over the last couple thousand years, the human race has been faced with its own emotional center and has been given the freedom to act upon it. This has a good side and a bad side. For example, marriage for the sake of love instead of for the sake of economics, politics, and breeding has become much more accepted over the past two millennia. Many cultures have done away with the tradition of arranged marriages allowing potential partners to discover their own reasons for marriage. Even those cultures which kept this tradition often now take into consideration the desires and feelings of the betrothed (when once they did not) and search for spousal candidates that will satisfy the need for love and emotional fulfillment along with the other benefits of arrangement. However, this freedom of selection has also vastly increased the number of divorces and the number of people in unhappy marriages, abusive partnerships, and other undesirable circumstances caused from a lack of emotional intelligence, lack of emotional strength and the indulgence of selfish emotions. Traditional marriages tend to avoid these pitfalls. Being granted the freedom to choose a partner requires a great deal of responsibility, self-awareness, honesty, integrity, self-love, and the ability to provide unconditional love to another person. Without all of these things, a relationship will end or stagnate one way or another.

We have also discovered within ourselves the urge to wage war based on belief. Wars in the ancient past were declared based on the prognostications of oracles and priests, generally not on whim or fanaticism. Over the last two thousand years, oracles became far less popular as Christianity outlawed the practices of trance-channeling and divination, so military and political leaders were left to listen to their own hearts and keep their own counsel on when to go to war and who to march against. This has led to a great many full scale and small scale wars being fought over feelings of hatred, anger, jealousy, vengeance, superiority, arrogance, family feuds and differences in religious beliefs. However, unlike in the ancient past, wars have been ended or even entirely prevented based on feelings of love, forgiveness, righteousness, justice, compassion, sympathy, empathy, forbearance, serenity and charity.

But how does an angry and vengeful king calm himself and sublimate his urge to rally the troops and march forth?

We can see the beginning of this way of thinking and acting emerging around the year 500_{BC} when the earliest hints of the Age of Pisces were beginning to bleed into the Age of Aries and cause a fundamental change within humanity. Prophets and thinkers such as Gautama Buddha, Lao Tzu, Seneca, and Zeno began teaching a new and effective way of dealing with life and suffering. The religious and philosophic movements and schools of ethics and behavior founded by these individuals have a great deal in common. Buddhism, Taoism, and Stoicism seem to have been inspired by the same spiritual impulse and paved the way for any individual to gain self-mastery without the need for ritual magic, propitiation of deities, ablutions, or entry into the mystery schools. All that these systems require is the ability to reflect inwardly on oneself.

Beginning with these practices is very simple. You start by using your intellect to convince yourself of an axiom:

You should not be bothered by the things which you cannot control.

As soon as you have convinced yourself that it is a waste of time and energy to experience the arousal of emotions caused by an external trigger that is out of your hands, you will find it much easier to remain centered and serene in all circumstances. If you cannot control what is happening, why feel any way about it? Why feel angry? Why feel happy? Why feel annoyed? Why feel elated? It is pointless and these emotions will pull you from your center and cause you to make decisions which will seem quite inadvisable once you have sobered up and centered yourself again. Have you ever made a decision out of anger and later realized that it will have terrible consequences? Have you ever made a decision or a plan out of happiness and elation only to later realize that it is actually quite a stupid thing that you would really rather not do?

This stage is all about using your mind to subdue your immature and unruly heart. I can hear the New Agers screaming, "Blasphemer! Heretic! The heart is more important than anything!" While it is true that consciousness and spirit enter this world through your heart and the heart is the primary source of a healthy, balanced and effective life, it is only such if it is clear and stable. If your heart is wracked by emotions and is moved hither, thither and yon on the choppy seas of everyday life and it is out of your control, then your heart is going to lead you astray. In this condition, it is not the great engine and beacon of spirit and light that you think it ought to be – it is more like a hormonal teenager.

Clarity comes from the mind. The mind is the primary source of logic. If you find that at times you are swept up in any feelings including anger, sadness, sentiment, joy, etc. and cannot control them, or find that you do not even want to control them, if you cannot make good decisions or think clearly in these states, it is because there is an immaturity within your heart or a trauma that needs to be recognized and healed. You must notice whenever you are swept up and away by emotions. Recognize it and declare to yourself that you recognize it. Then declare to yourself the intention to let the feeling arise and cease and pass away on its own. Do not fight it, do not struggle to control it, but set the intention that you eventually want to control it and for now you will just watch it, observe it, detach from it, prevent yourself from getting absorbed in it, and let it go.

After your heart has been subdued and made tame through a great deal of effort and practice which comes with the experience of everyday life, then you may again allow yourself to feel more freely. You will discover that you can actually control your emotions and choose which ones to feel and when. You will never achieve this control if you fail at using the coolness of your mind to quench the fires of your heart. As we go through life, every single day affords us opportunities to become annoyed, angry, vengeful, elated, excited, aroused, and so on. We must notice when these emotions arise then contemplate why they arose. Do not attempt to change them at first – just notice and observe. It will help to write down your observations in a journal. Every time you feel any emotion whatsoever, do your best to remember yourself, observe yourself and your surroundings, allow the feeling to persist at its own pace and be with it and follow it back within yourself to its origin.

At first, this will be difficult and strange. We never really think about where and how within our souls emotions arise; we simply unconsciously allow them to do whatever they want. But the same way a homing pigeon leaves a magnetic marker within its coop and will always find its way back home, your emotions also leave a similar marker when they fly off into the world of expression and it can be followed like a trail of breadcrumbs back to its source. Just breathe, close your eyes, breathe again, feel the emotion, feel your body. Is there some sensation happening in your stomach? Perhaps there is a feeling in your heart. Maybe its in your throat or up in your head. Are your ears getting warm? Is your jaw clenching? Maybe it is loosening. Are your toes curling? Are you tightening your fists? Our body can give us the first hints as to where these emotions arise.

Sensations in the feet can arise when one wants to stand their ground and fight, or perhaps when one wants to flee from danger, or when one feels stuck in an unfavorable situation. A person's ears and cheeks can become flushed and warm when embarrassed or during moments of romantic infatuation. Feelings in the chest or heart can be caused by genuine love and compassion, by depression and sadness, or by serious forms of anger and resentment. Minor forms of anger can cause the stomach to feel tight or abuzz with energy. This same center can be excited by nervousness, excitement and anticipation. And of course there can be simultaneous arousal of these centers and different mixtures of intensity, and some people have completely different centers aroused when feeling these emotions. Everyone is different.

This is where your journal will come in handy. Keep a record of the bodily sensations you feel and their associated emotions.

Also, and very importantly, keep track of the food you have been eating and what is currently in your stomach when making these observations. This may be quite illuminating and can help you select the diet that is correct for you if you notice that certain foods make you prone to certain emotions while other foods assist you in centering yourself.

Keep as much organized data about your self-observations as you can and after one to three years, you will very likely be able to perceive and collate patterns. These patterns are the fingerprint of your soul – your astral body. Your astral body is the root of your emotions and you can perceive its character, its personality, its signature, by recognizing its patterns of manifestation regarding emotion and instinct. Having this fingerprint is a significant milestone on your path to direct perception of your own soul. You will be more aware of it and its characteristics and anatomy. You will begin to see the different astral organs you possess and how each one of those organs is responsible for its own range of emotions. The same way you select healthy foods and medicines to nourish your various biological organs, and you understand which foods and which herbs are good for which organs, you will begin to select healthy thoughts and behaviors that nourish your astral organs. The more you do it, the more skilled you become and the easier it gets.

Do not force this process. Do not resist your emotions or suppress them (unless of course you are in public and do not want to make a scene or put innocent bystanders into the path of your fury!) When you have indigestion, you do not fight it and resist the pain, you drink some ginger tea. You must use your mind and your thoughts like a compassionate doctor to medicate your emotions. Spiritual self-medication comes from the mind. Do not become angry or disappointed when you fail at first, or if you should relapse later. Be kind with yourself, allow yourself to feel the emotions, allow them to arise and cease on their own if you cannot find the mental medicine for them. Simply noticing them intently is also a dose of medicine. It allows you to see how they arise and cease. Every time you use your powers of awareness to notice them, you have taken a step down the path, you have done one rep of weight training, you will have glimpsed another aspect of your astral body, and your mastery will grow and unfold in due time at its own pace.

The more you do this, the more you will become aware of your astral body, the more you will understand its mechanisms and the more you will be able to select those emotions you wish to feel and sublimate the ones you do not. You will become an expert at resisting all kinds of temptations because your thoughts will no longer be clouded by your emotions.

Another added benefit is that you will become extremely aware of how others manage in this regard. You will begin to see exactly what sort of emotionality they have and how far along the path of self-mastery they are. It will enhance your social life and public awareness immensely. It will also enable you to recognize when a person is attempting to manipulate your emotions in order to influence your thoughts, choices, beliefs and behavior. If you have ever wanted to become immune to propaganda, politicians, technologists trying to sell you something and charismatic charlatans and users of all sorts, this is exactly how.

***

These are our great tasks, our great initiations, in this Manvantara – to resist the temptation to take the quick and easy path to convenience, power and wealth through selfishness and cruelty, and instead practice forbearance, compassion and a clear intellect to expand the heart chakra and operate from that center. Practicing this heart-centered, mind-regulated thinking, feeling, and willing will provide one with the strength, confidence and capability of overcoming any of the lures of modern technology, trendy science, trendy spiritualism and political demagoguery – the tools of seduction used to lure people into the Eighth Sphere.

Transmogrification: The Appearance of Paranormal Phenomena

To understand the Eighth Sphere more fully, we must examine and contemplate our place in the universe and how our sense perceptions work. How much of reality can we perceive under normal circumstances? Do our sense organs provide us with an accurate representation of reality as it truly is? What aspects of reality remain hidden from us and how can we know what we do not directly perceive?

Questions such as these go largely unasked and unanswered in the world of modern science. Scientists rarely concern themselves with First Principles, the realm of Causes or epistemology. They are too concerned with studying the ephemeral effects of the phenomenal world. It is quite a bit easier and there is far more money in it. They also dislike running afoul of the High Priesthood of Academia when they accidentally discover something that goes against the prevailing dogma and paradigm. It is far better to count and catalog the scales on a river trout than to ask the question: "Why and how do I perceive this river trout? Who perceives this river trout? Who am I?"

Their brains generally begin to melt at this point. Panic sets in. The yawning abyss of their ignorance becomes painfully apparent as the gap between what they know and do not know is magnified to near infinity when they realize that they have no idea what their consciousness is or how to properly use it to study the world outside themselves. They are faced with the ontological dread that they have overlooked and neglected something so obvious and so close to themselves. "How could I be so blind? How can I use my perceptions and my mind for the pursuit of science if I do not even know what my perceptions or my mind are, let alone how they work?" They are thrown beyond the precipice, like Wiley Coyote running off the cliff, feeling like he is on solid ground until the moment he looks down and realizes he is thousands of feet in the air with no solid ground beneath him, a mere moment away from falling to his doom. The horror bursts forth from within as they witness their own fundamental stupidity and their ego is shocked into action which rushes in to defend itself and prevent the potential midlife crisis, nay, the personality dissolution that was so close to occurring, and they convince themselves that such inquiry is unimportant and unprofitable and they return to counting scales on fish, having quickly forgotten the Lovecraftian levels of insanity and cosmic terror that they just experienced.

But I imagine if you are holding and reading this book, you will be more than comfortable with strange inquiries that require unconventional thinking. You should feel right at home in this chapter as we explore the topics of sense-perception, parallel worlds and paranormal phenomena.

***

We must begin by admitting to ourselves that our five senses really are not all they are cracked up to be. Some like to think of them from a glass-half-full perspective, that our senses have developed through millions of generations of evolution and over time they improve and expand our ability to perceive reality. One could also take the opposite perspective and think of them as a limiter valve on consciousness. Without a body, a nervous system, or any senses, our consciousness is infinite and unlimited, encompassing all things while it is at one with the Mind of God. When we enter into the human experience and live as an individual, this infinite consciousness is limited by the human body and its sense organs. The expansive awareness shrinks down to a single point of awareness that perceives reality from one tiny human perspective.

It is our task to acknowledge both perspectives and not get stuck with either one. Indeed, infinite consciousness is limited by the human experience, but that should not stir within us any feelings of dread, disappointment or self-hatred. And indeed, our sense organs are wonderful, beautiful and mysterious and allow us to experience reality as a rich tapestry of wonder, but we should not be overly proud of ourselves especially considering that our senses actually do not perceive much phenomena at all.

Our ears can only detect sounds that range from roughly 20 Hertz to 20 Kilohertz. But there are of course frequencies far lower and far higher than this range. We know that dogs and cats can perceive high-pitched sounds that we cannot. We also know that most animals can feel extremely low vibrations that occur before an earthquake. They even sense fluctuations within the magnetosphere of which humans are largely oblivious.

Our eyes can only detect wavelengths of light ranging from roughly 400 nanometers to 700 nanometers. However, we know that the light spectrum range is far greater than this. There are radio waves of enormous size and slow vibration on the low end of the spectrum and it extends all the way up passed our sense-perceivable range to the realm of potent radioactivity like UV rays, X-rays, gamma rays, and the mysterious "cosmic rays" which are so difficult to detect and parse out even with modern machinery that we have used this umbrella term to describe an entire world of high-frequency radiation.

Regarding our other senses, we are able only to feel and come into contact with those things which have enough solidity to collide with our solid bodies or enough temperature, electromagnetism or flavor to excite our nerve-endings.

All-in-all, the physical sense organs of human beings are able to perceive less than two percent of the reality in which we live. And for now, that may be for the best. Most of us are like baby fish swimming in the relatively safe shallows near the shore, far away from any sharks, giant squids, and Leviathans. If at this point, our senses were enhanced and expanded, we might see some things that would make H.P. Lovecraft blush. Most people are startled when a squirrel runs by in the dark or when they see a tiny spider skitter across their desk. I can only imagine how some people would react to witnessing some of the other denizens of this vast universe which lurk in the invisible realms beyond sight and sound, but oh so close to us.

The entire range of the electromagnetic spectrum and the spectrum of all phenomena in the universe can be called the Superspectrum. This is a term coined by the journalist and paranormal researcher John Keel[10] of *The Mothman Prophecies* fame.

It was his theory that much of the paranormal phenomena that people experience are caused by things which originate in the ranges of the Superspectrum that we cannot perceive and entering into the range of the Superspectrum that we can perceive. For example, a common detail in the reports of many UFO's is that they seem to appear out of nowhere and have nebulous luminous features and a violet hue, and as they descend down toward the earth, they gain more solid-looking metallic features and move through the colors of the light spectrum from violet (the highest frequency of visible light) to red (the lowest frequency of visible light) and finally to a solid aluminum-looking object.

A thought experiment about multi-dimensional perception would be useful here. Imagine that you are a two-dimensional being. You live in 2Distan. You can only see lines of various lengths in front of you and nothing else. Three-dimensional shapes and bodies are beyond your ability to perceive or comprehend except for perhaps some very advanced thinkers and mystics in your little line world. But let us now imagine that a three dimensional body passes slowly through your world from above downward. This shape is a sphere. At first, you would witness a dot in front of you appearing out of seemingly nowhere and it would grow into a long line over time, then after a certain point, that line would shrink back down to a dot and disappear. All that you witnessed was a line that appeared, grew and shrank and then disappeared. But in reality, a ball just passed through your planar world. But you have absolutely no idea what a ball is. You have no frame of reference to even conceive of a ball. Your entire world is nothing but dots and lines. Only insane occultists, conspiracy theorists, drug users and religious kooks talk about balls and cubes and tetrahedra passing through your world. What a load of nonsense!

Now imagine you are you again, a perfectly normal three-dimensional human being. You discover this two-dimensional world and wish to dip your hand into it. As your first couple of fingertips enter 2Distan, the 2Distanis see one then two dots that grow into short lines but then cease growing. Then two more dots appear as your index and pinky fingers enter that quickly turn into two lines similar in length and stop growing. Then a fifth dot appears and lengthens into a slightly longer line than the rest as your thumb plunges in. These five lines then merge together into one long line as you are now palm-deep in this world. Then you retract your hand and the 2D people witness the long length divide into five lines, which shrink into little dots one-by-one and disappear. They have absolutely no comprehension of what just occurred. They are utterly flabbergasted. The newspapers are going wild, emergency service phones are ringing off the hook, the 2Distani government is attempting to cover it up and gaslight the witnesses while they scramble little line jets to chase your hand and then desperately create secret programs to study this strange phenomenon. Conspiracy theorists start talking about their line world being visited by lines from another line world who possess more advanced line technology. Your simple act of dipping your hand into a lower-dimensional world has certainly caused quite a stir!

I hope that this thought experiment is more than sufficient to aid you in realizing that "there are more things in Heaven and Earth, Horatio, than are dreamt of in your philosophy."[11]

It may prove fruitful to use this multi-dimensional lens to study what we refer to as UFO phenomena, poltergeists, cryptozoology, premonitions and other paranormal and parapsychological phenomena. I would find it amusing if some of the bizarre physics-defying behavior of certain UFO's could be explained as a higher-dimensional hand waving hello. Simply because these things appear like spaceships to us, does that mean we should take them at face value?

***

Consider now the so-called "contacts" from the 1950's in which hapless humans were visited by alleged "space brothers" from Venus who looked just like quintessential Aryan human beings. By the 1970's when astronomers and astrophysicists realized that Venus is a very inhospitable planet, these "aliens" started to tell their contactees that they were now hailing from the Pleiades, and nary a visitor from Venus was seen again. Very convenient. I bet they hoped no one would notice.

The details of these contact events are interesting to consider. For instance, George Adamski, arguably the world's most famous contactee, was visited by a being named Orthon[12]. This reminded me of elementary school math class. An orthogonal line is a line which is perpendicular to another. An orthogonal plane is a plane which is perpendicular to another. The beginning of the study of hyper-dimensional mathematics (a system of mathematics that deals in higher and lower dimensions) requires use of the concept that each higher dimension is orthogonal to the dimension beneath it. It is odd that this being's name shares an etymological root with this concept of multi-dimensionality.

Another famous case is that of Howard and Connie Menger of High Bridge, New Jersey[13] (a "bridge" to a "higher" dimension perhaps? Always be on the look-out for patterns in toponymy and nomenclature!) They claimed to be in regular contact with the Venusians during the 1950's to the 1970's and even took photos of sketches of their spacecraft! Howard made appearances on the *Long John Nebel* radio show, which was the precursor to Art Bell's *Coast to Coast AM* radio show, which was the precursor to everyone's favorite *Info Wars* with Alex Jones.

Howard and Connie became friends with a Venusian named Valiant Thor, our world's most famous and public space brother. During a contactee gathering at the Menger farm in rural New Jersey which included many participants claiming to have been visited by beings from space, the charismatic and handsome Valiant Thor himself showed up and introduced himself to the crowd. He is said to have been able to speak any language, he had no finger prints, and he could walk through walls. And to top it off, he was the Commander of all Venusians stationed on Earth. (It is noteworthy that throughout history, normal human beings who were trained adepts of occult orders were reported to have these exact same characteristics and abilities. Just saying.)

Allegedly, Thor would go on to meet with top officials of the United States government including President Dwight Eisenhower, Vice President Richard Nixon, the Undersecretary of Defense, the head of the Central Intelligence Agency, and the Joint Chiefs of Staff. His message to them was the same as all Venusian and Pleiadean messages to essentially every contactee who has ever spoken with them:

> "Please don't blow up any nukes.
>
> The Cold War is stupid.
>
> Don't pollute the environment.
>
> Play nice with each other."

This is sensible advice. Thanks space brothers! Much appreciated!

Do we really need some alien from another world to tell us these things? A quick ping from our conscience should be sufficient to accommodate all of the above, don't you think?

Well, maybe those sociopaths in D.C. need to hear things like this because Lord knows their mama and daddy didn't teach 'em.

But a healthy, well-adjusted, normal human being with a conscience should readily understand that it is in bad form to vaporize people with mega weapons and to defecate where they dine, and that being kind to each other is simply baseline common sense. Perhaps that is all Valiant Thor, the Venusians, and the Pleiadeans really are: symbolic representations of our conscience or "higher selves" from a higher dimension that showed up in tangible form to a number of good old boys who grew up stuffing their mouths with Cracker Jacks and their minds with pulp sci-fi comics. Valiant Thor perfectly fit their expectations and their frame of reference to provide just the right amount of familiarity while maintaining an air of mystery and authority to get people to listen to him, be enamored of him, and to heed his words. Our collective conscience about the Cold War and industrial society was being ignored and repressed so it produced an egregore, a thought form, a psychic compensation with physical attributes.

(Or perhaps some very talented occultists decided it was time to masquerade as aliens from other worlds and tell people how they think a healthy society should operate. No one would listen to them if they introduced themselves as musicians and plumbers from New Jersey who know some occult science. But, hey! An alien from Venus or the Pleiades! There's some authoritativeness! The important thing here is to take not at face value the illusory, unclear and the psychically potent and culturally timely attributes of this sort of phenomena. This will provide us with some insights into how the Eighth Sphere functions.)

***

Psychic compensation is a theory dreamt

up by 20th century psychologist Carl Gustav Jung in his reveries about UFO's. Indeed he wrote a book about UFO's called *Flying Saucers*[14]. Now Carl Jung did not really dream up this theory in an original sense. It is a repackaging of a ritual magic operation in which the magician creates a physical manifestation of something he is thinking, feeling or willing into existence. The manifestation is called a thought form, an elementary, an egregore, or to the Tibetans, a kulpa or sprulpa (mistranslated as "tulpa" by the Theosophical Society. So if you use the word "tulpa," I will know where you got your information and I will give you a disapproving head shake and raise my eyebrow at you.)

A sprulpa is a physical manifestation of the Buddha sent to people who need to be taught some important lesson.

An egregore generally only comes into existence when the operator really wants or needs it to. It is a physical manifestation of a repressed emotional or psychological need. This is why Carl Jung calls it a compensation; it is compensating for a need that goes unrecognized or unfulfilled. Sometimes this need is so strong that if it continues to be repressed and unfulfilled, it will burst forth into physical reality and can appear in the most outrageous and fantastical way, expending all of the pent-up psychic energy in a way that defies explanation and cannot be ignored any longer by the person or people who have so expertly ignored and repressed it up to this point. Something non-material like an emotion or a fear is easy to ignore, but something material can literally give you a wake-up call, slap you in the face, and provide you with a nice sunburn at midnight (as many UFO's are wont to do.)

Jung reported that a person who has suffered the loss of a loved one but was unable or refused to grieve is likely to experience UFO encounters or dreams involving this deceased loved one. The deceased would show up in a luminous circular object (circles being a psychic symbol of wholeness and completion) and communicate messages of love, forgiveness, and letting go. Jung also reported that people who feel extremely disappointed with this world, perhaps they are downtrodden, or they dislike the physical and emotional suffering experienced by humans, or maybe the government is too oppressive for their taste, or the economic system feels like a slave system, or some other type of problem that they cannot emotionally bare, will experience visitation from alien beings who live on other worlds which have governments, economies and lifestyles that are Utopian in comparison to the Earth. The book and movie *K-PAX* by, Gene Brewer comes to mind.

A world which has sunken to the depths

of materialism and anti-spiritual thinking, much like our own modern culture, may experience compensation for the lack of spirituality. The natural, inborn need to experience spiritual awakening and a connection to the source of reality is stifled to awful extents in our world and people's hearts are in agony over this. The religious institutions have failed to fulfill this need. The scientific pursuit has failed to fulfill this need. The New Age movement does its best, but good Lord, let's not open that can of worms. The Eastern "gurus" are almost all frauds or are operating from a loose collection of nebulous mystical half-truths. The various ideologies and political movements which prey upon confused and directionless people seeking meaning in their lives have not only failed to supply this need, but have caused more strife than can be quantified.

The religious groups turned their backs on deep spirituality dubbing it evil and divergent and deriding and chastising any who practice it to be worshiping the devil or communing with demons. The scientists did the same to spirituality, the only difference is that they dubbed it unreal and illusory. And the groups who have rediscovered some inkling of the true way have become so lost in subjective mysticism or have only discovered such a small piece of the puzzle that their findings are of little use to newcomers wishing to start down their spiritual path.

The Tradition has been driven underground to the point of near destruction, at least on the material plane, so when people feel that spark in their soul, when they hear that calling in their heart and realize that they need to find a higher and deeper meaning in life, there is almost nothing available for them. No help comes from incarnated people. No great spiritual initiators or gurus are offering their assistance except in very rare and intimate circumstances and in very small groups. So few authentic spiritual masters exist today. Spiritual seekers are on their own, left to figure it out by their lonesome, lost in a sea of self-help charlatans, wine-drinking, crystal gripping Tarot readers, Western mystics from Los Angeles drenched in Eastern regalia in their yoga studios, tent revivalists shouting about damnation, mall goth ritual magicians covered in Thelema-themed jewelry, UFO cults promising a better future, priests trying to convince them that everything they need is in some old book, or New Thought manifestation specialists telling people what they already know and charging a premium for it. Most seekers will not succeed. There are many seeds cast by the wayside on stones and sterile dirt; so little fertile soil is left.

I know that I am being cynical. There are some great people with an enormous capacity to teach and share their gifts and insight. But that does not change the fact that walking the spiritual path today is incredibly confusing, arduous, lonely, difficult and chock-full of pitfalls that most people never overcome. In a traditional and healthy civilization, there are institutions populated by a number of fully advanced spiritual masters who could, in actual fact, initiate you into the spiritual mysteries by the passing on of their spiritual energies and knowledge if you became inclined to have that experience. These institutions are public and readily available in a traditional society. No such institutions exist today. There are plenty of institutions, societies, and groups who pretend to offer this service or wish they could, but who in fact are providing essentially nothing (will the real Freemasonry please stand up?) Generally the only people who are spiritually awakened today are those who were born awakened or those who have persevered in discovering and collecting countless stale breadcrumbs which acted as vague signposts to a potential spiritual goal and were diligent and forthright enough in their discernment and discipline to actually achieve a spontaneous awakening through hard work and the grace of God. Initiation really only comes from a suprahuman source today. (But perhaps this is a blessing in disguise. Those who are sufficiently prepared for spiritual initiation will find it coming directly to them from a Divine source and may not need membership in any sort of fraternity or institution.)

It is no wonder why there is so much paranormal phenomena in our modern world! Our spiritual yearning is being collectively suppressed and diverted. Large portions of the human population are creating compensations – egregores – in the form of UFO's with spiritually advanced occupants or trance-channeled spirit guides giving them messages of seeming prophetic importance that are really just repackaged spiritual facts that can be discovered through self-awareness training or by leafing through *The New Testament* or *Tao te Ching*. There are poltergeists, premonitions, UFO encounters, visions of saints and deities, and so on, likely illusory, although physically real, and almost certainly caused by an unfulfilled need for spirituality. According to Buddhist tradition, a sprulpa will appear to someone who is in dire psychological need of a wake up call.

Or at least this is one theory – one possibility – that may aide in demystifying a portion of paranormal events.

***

Perhaps I should sprinkle in a healthy dose of materialism for the left-brained readers to make the above slightly more palatable.

Sulfur is one of the main ingredients in nitrogen fixation in organic systems along with iron and molybdenum. This means that it helps an organism take nitrogen from the atmosphere and convert it into ammonia which is then used to build amino acids, proteins, alkaloids, DNA and RNA[15]. It is generally part of the first stage of creating a material body for an organism. It also smells like stinky egg farts; a common complaint among witnesses of paranormal activity.

Sometimes flying saucers that are parked in the woods or a field somewhere smell of sulfur. Bigfoot is also said to leave a lingering trail of this odor wherever he goes. Ghosts, apparitions and demons throughout the ages have been reported to wreak of this aroma. It is one of the reasons that people associate Hell with sulfur (a.k.a. brimstone) – the demons that have been spotted mowing the wheat fields or harassing the unrepentant have always been in dire need of a bath or a less egg-rich diet.

UFO's, Bigfoot, demons, aliens, ghosts, and apparitions all have another thing in common: they never stick around very long. They are here one minute and gone the next. Occasionally they leave traces behind – strange goo or a sticky pile of silicates sometimes referred to as ectoplasm by spiritualists that will cause numbness in your fingers should you reach out and touch it, gossamer strands of an unknown substance that will vanish within a few days, or patches of parched soil that will not support plant life for months or even years after the event. That is all that will be left by large metallic objects with strange occupants. Sometimes nothing at all is left behind and the object simply vanishes from sight in an instant without a sound as though it was never there. Many times they do not fly away as reported, they simply are no longer there in the blink of an eye. There have been countless witnesses to "spaceship" phenomena who have reported watching it take off and fly away only to recant years later, believing they would have sounded as though they were hallucinating had they told the truth that the object and its occupants simply blinked out of existence and left behind the lingering odor of hard-boiled eggs.

Jacques Vallée[16] and F.W. Holiday[17] have reported that the elusive Bigfoot is elusive for a very good reason. He, too, vanishes in short order after appearing. Hunters have found his large and famous footprints coming to sudden stops in the middle of large, open fields with nothing but a very small smattering of goo left on the ground. These reports are largely ignored by the producers of those made-for-TV documentaries about Bigfoot hunters. The prevailing theory is that he is a normal large primate who is the reigning Hide-and-Seek World Champion. But what if he was something else entirely? What if these phenomena are literally appearing out of thin air? The stench of sulfur may be a clue that these entities appear by creating proteins and organic bodies for themselves using the abundant nitrogen of our atmosphere.

When something comes into material existence for a limited amount of time through occult processes and again vanishes, this is known as transmogrification. This has long since been the goal of many occult practices and religious ceremonies. There are tales, fables, scriptures and grimoires teeming with such accounts and instructions. Considering that most of these old books were written by fully developed adult men with strong literary comprehension and communication skills and a deep appreciation of natural science and philosophy – some of these men were even high status court members, revered hermits, respected professors at universities and bishops of the Church – we can assume they had at least a passable grasp on reality and were relatively sane, and yet, they wrote of such things that today are ridiculed by so-called "educated" people. And their books are in such agreement with each other from culture to culture and era to era that it makes one wonder if these individuals had actual success with these operations.

Many of these grimoires contain some dark and uncouth instructions regarding the blood and life forces of animals or even people.

Animal and human sacrifice has been a staple in the spirit-summoning arts for millennia. There were even cultures who practiced open-air public sacrifices of humans and animals in an attempt to not only appease, but to summon their gods. There were temples that looked like they were made by or for giants adorned with enormous golden thrones replete with golden dishware in places like Baalbek and Teotihuacan. Is it so difficult to imagine that these priests hoped to provide enough blood and life force for their "thirsty gods"[18] to manufacture organic bodies for themselves and to sit in these enormous thrones? Is it also a coincidence that the three main ingredients of nitrogen fixation are found in the ritual implements of these occult operations which are said to summon physical creatures? Blood is rich in iron and magicians would use sulfur powder or sulfur incense often burned in a lead dish, however; original magical lead was called *malybdos* by the ancient Greeks and may have in fact been molybdenum and not lead at all.

Gold is a favored metal among temple priests possibly due to its incredibly dense molecular structure. It is believed to be dense enough that if a seat, a ritual implement, or other item were made from it, the gods in all their subtlety would be able to sit upon it or physically interact with it, unlike other materials which they would pass right through.

Apparently a little blood goes a long way, especially for Bigfoot. Whenever there are reports of a Squatch stealing animals from an unsuspecting farmer or homesteader, the reported missing animals are usually just one chicken out of an entire coop, or one small dog on a farm with larger dogs. Would a massive primate such as one fitting the description of Bigfoot not require far more than one chicken per day to sustain itself? And if there were so many chickens which were so easy to steal, why did only one go missing?

Perhaps one is all it takes for that particular transmogrification to be successful. After all, the average encounter of a Bigfoot lasts no longer than a few minutes.

***

It is my hope that the transmogrification theory will be examined further by researchers. The "Extraterrestrial Hypothesis" (or ETH) is based on some faulty reports. Many of the reported objects do not in fact fly in from or take off back into space. They seem to simply blink into and out of our reality. This of course does not preclude extraterrestrial visitation, but it does indeed weaken the ETH as a whole in many circumstances.

The nitrogen fixation process reminds me of the process of building the Eighth Sphere that

Rudolf Steiner discussed. Drawing matter away from the earth to create a pseudo-world of phantasms certainly smacks of transmogrification. Perhaps this is where some of these paranormal phenomena come and go. But where does this pseudo-world get its inspiration? How does it choose the shapes and appearances of its phenomena?

In their book, *Origins of the Gods*[19], Andrew Collins and Gregory Little discuss some of their findings regarding the legendary Uintah Basin, home of the famous Skinwalker Ranch in Utah. Something that they had mentioned reminded me of the great "chicken or the egg" scenario. That area has been home to shamanic ritual for time immemorial. Perhaps because these shamans were aware of paranormal phenomena that would occur so often there. Or perhaps these shamans created this "power place" intentionally, causing a rift to form between worlds and allowing paranormal irruptions to frequent this location. It is difficult to know. One such phenomenon is the appearance of wolfmen, or werewolves. Creatures between five and seven feet tall that walk on two legs but have lupine features have been reported to be seen in the Basin for centuries. We also have historical records from the 19th century of shamans performing rituals in the Basin wearing wolf skins and heads as regalia.

Were these shamans mimicking the wolfmen which they may have seen haunting this territory? Or is the Superspectrum mimicking the shamans? Perhaps the shamans left an imprint on the Superspectrum and it reproduced the shape and behavior of the shamans, but not accurately. The Superspectrum may produce poor copies of real phenomena or of things pulled from the human psyche. This may explain some of the stranger paranormal reports regarding landed flying saucers and their occupants that look like they are wearing bad costumes from 1950's science fiction films. Rectangular robots that beep and wobble from side to side as they walk, tiny green people with fishbowl helmets, human-looking aliens with outfits made of shiny metallic material like Mylar, and many other just plain stupid things have come out of round metal "spaceships" that look more at-home on a Hollywood movie set or in a pulp fiction comic book than in the cockpit of a spacecraft. UFO witnesses have also been visited and threatened in their homes by alleged military officers who had simple-minded bizarre personalities and similar names and features to actual officers at nearby bases – similar, but not the same – like cheap copies of real people[20].

It is also interesting to note that such reports exist only from the 1950's to the 1970's. After that, there seem to be no more goofy-looking movie props coming out of spaceships. I have searched a few thousand encounter reports to discover if there are any recent visitations with Hollywood extras but have found none dating any later than the 1970's. Either the so-called "Little Grays," the praying mantis people, and the Pleiadeans took over the tourism industry for planet Earth and kicked everyone else out, or the phenomenon has simply adopted a new mask.

Jacques Vallée discusses this at length in his research. The phenomenon changes its appearance depending on the culture and people with whom it interacts. At one point in the remote past, it showed up as religious deities, fairies, sprites, and semi-spiritual nobility. In the late medieval era, it presented itself as flying ghost ships replete with sails and anchors scraping against the ground, mere decades before people would begin building such caravels and establishing the Age of Exploration. Then it began showing itself as blimps and zeppelins in the 1890's with engineering crews clad in overalls speaking about traveling around the world. These zeppelins looked almost exactly like the ones humans would be building a decade later, however; these ones could fly as fast as a speeding bullet! After this, it began digging through the old costume warehouses in Hollywood studio lots just a decade before the Space Age was inaugurated. And recently it has been appearing as little bald gray-skinned people with large black eyes who want to create human-gray hybrids just before the medical industry began tampering with humans and our DNA. Apparently these grays are in league with the Nordic-looking people and some tall praying mantis types. They are often seen together in the same "spaceships" and "medical examination rooms."

This particular type of paranormal phenomena – encounters with beings that appear to be from the sky or another world – actually has little consistency over time (despite what some talking heads on a certain popular TV show will tell you.) It seems to adapt itself to the expectations of human beings, but also can manipulate the expectations of human beings by appearing to be something new and novel. It appears as though it has the power to condition entire populations with new beliefs or to persuade them to develop new technologies like caravels, zeppelins, spaceships, or genetic modifications.

In fact, Rudolf Steiner warned that Ahriman wants to teach humans how to build all the technology they will ever invent as quickly as possible. Instead of allowing humans to develop at their own pace and allowing their minds and souls to keep up with developments in technology, Ahriman wants rapid technical advancements that will blindside humanity and allow him to gain influence over us by tricking people into using technologies that they are not spiritually mature enough to operate thereby giving him a foothold over our thinking, feeling and willing powers. It is my guess that much of our modern technology, particularly the silicon wafer microchip, has entered into the human world with the assistance of an entity such as Ahriman. Lieutenant Colonel Philip Corso in his book *The Day After Roswell* claims that this technology and many others besides came from recovered alien spacecraft[21]. Also, John Keel theorized along these lines in his *Why UFOs: Operation Trojan Horse*[22]. He believed that some entity, either from another planet or from the Eighth Tower and the Superspectrum, is using us as a womb to develop along their lines instead of our own. They purposely seeded our planet with crashed flying saucers with recoverable items which could be reverse-engineered and introduced into our world and widely sold on the open market. Perhaps, when enough of this alien technology is put into use and our infrastructure becomes dependent on it, this alien presence will have enough power and resources to conquer us unawares.

This phenomenon not only influences us technologically, but also mentally, politically, and culturally. Ahriman is not only interested in science and technology, but wherever there is rigid, inflexible dogma, there you will find his influence.

When Constantine sacked Rome, he could not decide what the official state religion should be until one night, he and his soldiers witnessed a large luminous cross lighting up the sky and Constantine heard a voice in his head speaking in Latin, "In hoc signo vinces" - "In this sign you shall conquer." He decided then and there that Christianity would be the official religion of his new Empire.

The Vedas are filled to the brim with stories of deities flying around in their otherworldly aircraft called vimanas and visiting people on the earth and encouraging them to start a new government, invade a certain nation, spread a new spiritual practice, spread a new dogma, or any number of other activities.

In the *Old Testament*, Nebuchadnezzar was asked by a voice in his head to construct a giant landing pad for YHWH's aerial chariot. After witnessing this thunderous and luminous cloud of golden light with a throne in its midst upon which sat a large human-looking entity with blue skin, Nebuchadnezzar was told by this being to invade Jerusalem and spare no one. Interestingly enough, this same entity – or at least a very similar one – had visited the prophet Ezekiel some years earlier and told him to preach to the people of Jerusalem and warn them that if they did not change their evil ways, turn toward YHWH and repent, a foreign army would despoil them of their lives and land[23].

***

I hope that this chapter has made it clear that the tired old Extraterrestrial Hypothesis is really not a very good place to start when researching this subject. Am I saying that aliens do not exist? Absolutely not. I have no idea whether they do or do not. I imagine that there is enough room in the universe for more people on more planets. However; that does not mean I am going to take UFO and "alien" encounters at face value. We live in a world full of trickery and deception and we must not ignore the Mercurial aspects of paranormal phenomena or fail in researching it from all angles. After all, the 8th Sephirah (Sphere) in the Kaballah tradition is the realm of Mercury, also called Hod. It is said to be the home of the gods and its dark side is known as the house of illusions.

The False Light

Ahriman preys upon confusion, ignorance, inflexible dogmatic thinking, lack of discernment and cognitive weaknesses of all kinds. He readily offers false knowledge – false light – whenever he sees an opportunity. Wherever there is rigid belief and stubborn perspective, there you will find Ahriman. Wherever there is unquestioned dogma which is forbidden to doubt, there you will find Ahriman. You will find Ahriman in equal measure under the vaulted ceilings of a church, in the hallowed halls of academia, or in the hotel conference rooms rented out for New Age conventions. He can be found in the hearts and minds of any number of priests, professors, and politicians. No institution is immune to his influence. Whenever things become calcified or ossified, when rigor mortis sets in either literally or figuratively, wherever change and fluidity meets resistance, the influence of Ahriman is present.

Many of us go to church on Sunday or synagogue on Saturday or mosque on Friday in an attempt to avoid the clutches of the devil, but many of us unwittingly walk right into his arms in these places. You will hear Ahriman speaking with another's lips whenever someone says something such as, "Our religion is the only true religion. This way is the only way. All other ways are evil and all other people are lost to damnation until they believe and accept what we believe and accept!"

Many of us go to school and study the allegedly unbiased discipline of modern science only to discover the same lack of freedom to question the theories presented to us. If a student doubts the prevailing dogma, they will fail the class. If a university student disagrees with the current paradigm's social ideologies and scientific theories, they are rendered unemployable. They may also be chastised, ostracized or ridiculed in some cases simply for thinking independently – I am speaking from personal experience.

In fact, in today's world, the wiser a person is, the lower their social status may be[24]. The wisest and most spiritually advanced people are generally cast out of society – either voluntarily or involuntarily – and are not permitted to benefit from it or participate in it. Generally speaking, only those who are obedient to the mainstream paradigm and believe in falsehoods are given wealth, employment opportunities, social selection, and political access. If a person lives in the truth and speaks the truth and is spiritually well-developed, they will rapidly find their opportunities for wealth, sex, friendship, family and political access evaporating before their very eyes. Of course there are exceptions to this rule, but think about it: how many saints, yogis, shamans, and self-possessed, self-aware, self-controlled people devoted to spirituality are the CEO's of billion-dollar corporations or are even basic salaried middle class types? The number approaches zero.

Now think about how many people there are who do not know their feet from their hands, believe every lie the government and news media tell them, accept every misrepresentation and falsehood taught to them in school, never question a single thing that is in front of them, possess a number of anti-spiritual thought patterns, regularly use lies and deception in every social circumstance and consider it to be perfectly normal and ethical, are convinced that selfishness is a virtue, believe that dating around like they are shopping for a new pair of shoes is somehow healthy and fair, and are seemingly on some form of human autopilot. All of these people have salaried jobs, active sex lives, plenty of social selection and political access, and are happy as clams[25].

Now look at me with a straight face and tell me that something is not deeply wrong with our civilization. The worst people rise to the top and the best people are trampled and spit upon. The most intelligent and wisest people generally decide not to have children, or have only very few, while the least healthy and most selfish people breed like gerbils. The most traitorous and diabolical personalities are rewarded with the most power and money for stabbing people in the back – sometimes literally – and despoiling the world of its dignity, freedom, and resources while the most conscientious, generous and selfless people are left to starve in poverty and are exploited by everyone around them for their kindness. Those who dedicate their lives to money will have wonderful and rich life-experiences while those who dedicate their lives to spirituality and self-development will be met with the worst hardships imaginable simply because they don't give a damn about money. The game has been rigged by a relatively small number of psychopaths who want to keep everyone who is unlike themselves in chains and in poverty. Extroverts are amply rewarded for indulging their most obnoxious and egoistic characteristics and essentially doing nothing of value for our culture while introverts are severely punished and chastised for trying to add things of great value to our culture. Introverts are generally pioneers of new fields but are punished and meet great resistance when paving new roads and will live and die in poverty and ridicule while Johnny-Come-Lately extroverts will later walk the road paved by an introvert as soon as it is socially acceptable to do so, stealing the ideas of the introvert and gaining all of the wealth, fame and credit that the introvert deserved while undergoing none of the struggle or sacrfice or possessing anywhere near the degree of knowledge, creativity and wisdom as the introvert. (We call these Johnny-Come-Latelies "sociopaths" in subculture theory. Whenever you see a famous internet personality who is making good money by speaking on a political, cultural or spiritual topic, there is a near perfect chance that they are a "sociopath" - a lukewarm grifter appealing to mass consciousness who understands the topic about as a deeply as a high schooler, just deeply enough to convince half-wits that they are intelligent, and will move on once the money dries up or the paradigm shifts again. These people creating an illusion of expertise are very much aligned with the Eighth Sphere and its propensity for falseness and ego gratification, particularly through the inhuman barrier of ego protective communications technology where dissidence, dissent, verification and falsification can be easily censored and drowned out.)

Introverts are told that if they wish to be "successful" they must act like extroverts while extroverts are told that introversion will lead to failure in life and is a symptom of various mental disorders newly invented for the new edition of the *Diagnostic and Statistical Manual of Mental Disorders*. Year after year, more and more spiritual characteristics are being labeled as mental disorders by the establishment. Rudolf

Steiner even warned that this would happen in a lecture in 1917 when he prophesied that spiritual inclinations would soon be looked upon as mental aberrations and that a vaccine would be developed which would eliminate all inclinations toward spirituality from a human being[26].

Everything is upside-down. Everything is backwards. What should be on the bottom is on top and what should be on top is on the bottom. The natural hierarchy has been overturned. What is good is seen as evil and what is in fact evil is seen as good.

These low-vibration conditions are necessary for the creation of the Eighth Sphere. Without these conditions, too few people would fall for the trap. But in the midst of such darkness, many will be led astray into the abyss of hedonism and ignorance that characterizes the realm of the Eighth Sphere.

***

When something is amiss in a person's life, they have three paths before them: seek contentment and freedom within oneself despite the outside world or attempt to alter the outside world to be more in line with their desires.

The third path is to strike a balance between these first two options. However, the first path of inner freedom must always take precedent and come before the second path can even be attempted, otherwise the person's life will be thrown out of balance and into chaos, misfortune, and illusion. If a person begins changing the outer aspects of their lives and the world around them before having gained a very high degree of spiritual wisdom, they will make enormous mistakes and create disharmonious conditions. They are not wise enough to know how to change their lives. They will create more problems than they solve when they begin altering and moving things around.

Gurdjieff describes this problem in his self-awareness training lessons. A person, the entire world, and everything that exists are all in perfect balance with each other. If someone decides to change one aspect of themselves without understanding how it is holistically connected to all other aspects of reality and how it will affect them, then they will not solve their troubles at all, but may in fact create new ones. Or they may perceive an undesirable circumstance as a problem and attempt to be rid of it when in fact it is an essential part of their life path that will lead to fulfillment and advancement.

Modern people and the modern science and political ideologies to which they subscribe do not care one iota about any of this. Most modern people do not really believe in an inner world. They tend to think of themselves as a collection of chemicals and molecules and nothing more. When something goes wrong in their life or in society, they never think, "How can I deal with this spiritually or psychologically? How can I see this from another perspective? Where is the blessing in disguise here? How can I use this as an opportunity to grow in spirit?" Instead, it becomes their mission to change the world until it no longer causes them discomfort or displeasure. And when they meet resistance to their agenda from other people, even more discomfort and displeasure erupts within them. Now not only do they have a problem with some condition of the world, but they have acquired enemies who disagree with their views or their solution. Before they can solve the perceived problem, they must first eliminate their enemies. Once they attempt to silence, defeat, or eliminate their enemies, they will create new problems because of these actions against humanity and the cycle begins anew with a fresh set of problems stacked on top of the old ones which remain unsolved.

  I hope you can see how this way of dealing with the world's problems has never, can never and will never succeed. It is a fallacy. And yet, it is how most people in this world think and act. Do not become paralyzed by these words. There is always a time for action, for outward-facing manipulation of the world, but only after a great deal of self-awareness training, exploring and conquering your inner world and awakening the dormant wisdom found within. There are very few leaders in this world, which is normal and natural. Few are capable of true free action, but everyone has the potential to become capable. Everyone has the potential to wear the mantle of leadership, however extremely rare it may be.

All of this corruption and degeneracy is a symptom of the inversion of the natural hierarchy of civilization. Society naturally divides itself into four castes; no matter what type of government a culture has or what types of ideologies it believes in, this always happens because it is natural and correct. However, it can be prevented from happening in a natural and correct manner when changes in conditions are forced upon the people and their minds are altered in some way skewing their objectivity and perverting their desires, or they prefer to disbelieve in the castes and each person considers oneself to be a special little snowflake. Modern people deny this because they believe in things that they call "progress," "equality" and "democracy" and equate success, freedom, power and status with money: the more wealth you possess, the higher your status. This is erroneous modern thinking and has no place in a normal, healthy mind. However, the fact remains that humanity consists of four castes which are as follows: The Aristocracy, The Military, The Economic Caste, and The Masses. This is the order of primacy in which they exist in a traditional and healthy civilization.

And of course there is a secret and small fifth caste whom we may call the Culture Bearers who exist outside, within, between, and beyond the other four castes. These are the truly awakened and inspired individuals who never find a place in any type of civilization – regardless how traditional or nontraditional – yet they are responsible for creating and developing the ideas, arts, philosophies, sciences, and spiritual disciplines that become the very lifeblood of a culture. They are simultaneously pariah and king, reviled and celebrated, outsider and insider, fool and confidante.

In a traditional society, the Aristocracy functions as the only caste with political power and any ideas of democracy are modulated by the fact that the Masses cannot possibly be sovereign as a group in general and the Military and Economic castes have no need for political access because their duty is to follow orders and carry out the mission of the Aristocracy. Individuals from the Masses can prove themselves worthy of rising through the castes and acquiring Economic, Military, or Aristocratic status just as anyone from a higher caste can prove themselves unworthy or incapable of holding that position and slip downward through the castes. This sort of meritocracy has always been a hallmark of long-lasting stable civilizations and a general principle of common sense within humanity as a whole. One does not require money to move up the hierarchy; one needs spiritual and personal development – character and reputation. Few people, even amongst the most ignorant, will disagree with this sentiment. Those who disagree are likely very lousy people who seek power and status through the acquisition of wealth or the commission of misdeeds.

Let me be clear. The Aristocracy in the Traditional definition are not simply "a group of the richest people." I am sure that many readers define "aristocracy" and the power elite as those who possess the most money. Again, this is only in the condition of today's modern degenerate dark age. The Aristocracy in an actual civilization that is worthy of the name "civilization" are the wisest and most spiritually advanced initiates of the occult Tradition. They are spiritual adepts of the highest order. They recognize each other through their enhanced perceptions and can see the spiritual qualities of any given person due to their high level of initiatic experience and intuition. In this way, there is no room for corruption in government. They will spot a traitor or a thief from a mile away. These types of people actually do in fact know what is best for humanity and society and so do not require democratic oversight for their policy-making. I know that this may be difficult for you to imagine or accept because many politicians today are thieves, degenerates, opportunists and murderers, while the decent politicians are forced to play along with these dirty games, and this is your frame of reference. But imagine that people like Jesus Christ or Shivananda or Lao Tzu or Buddha or Osiris or Krishna were the politicians in your government, and now imagine telling them that you know better than they and that they are making an error in judgment when writing laws – that they need democratic accountability. The presumption is absurd. Check your ego at the door. Do you really believe that they require democratic oversight or are you simply looking to gain political power for yourself?

You may consider this to be idealistic and naive, but I would argue that you are thinking from your mental conditioning, from your brainwashing – if you will excuse the term. If you have gone through the public education system or even a private education system, you have almost certainly been taught to hate the caste system and deny its existence despite the fact that you live in one. A shoemaker is not a banker and a banker is not a soldier and a soldier is not a yogi and a yogi is not a politician. The caste system is very real and it exists right now.

You are part of it and have a place in it. But you are told to hate it. You are told to deny it. You have never seen a properly functioning government or society. You may not be able to conceive of what one looks like, and I do not blame you. There are certainly none in our modern era. There are almost none in our history books – and the ones which are there are slandered for being illiberal and pre-modern, and everything illiberal and pre-modern is considered evil. Truly healthy societies may only be glimpsed in mythical accounts when a single God-King (or lineage of God-Kings who shared a single name or title – their similarity of reign, purpose and behavior so acute that distinction was unnecessary) would rule uninterrupted for thousands of years without so much as a protest against cabbage prices. There are scant historical accounts of such kings for two reasons: many existed long ago and the ones with good documentation had reigns so peaceful and boring that there is not much on which it is worth spending ink and paper. The sad truth is that the greatest kings who ever lived usually have less than a paragraph dedicated to them in our annals:

"The King was a wise man. He loved his wife and his wife loved him. Their children were well-behaved and well-loved by the masses. The soil was fertile and the farmers were respected and enjoyed their work and were well-paid. The economists were fair and everyone prospered.

The noble warriors protected the people and there were no abuses of violence thanks to the wonderful example set by the honorable aristocratic caste." This certainly doesn't make for a best-seller historical novel or a sexy Netflix series. History classes in universities called *Eras of Peace and Stability* would put nary a butt in a seat. The only students enrolled are there to catch up on their sleep.

But I ask that you entertain the possibility – even if only for a moment – that such myths and scant accounts are factually true. This thought exercise will transform the way you conceive of future possibilities. It may even unlock the endless well of optimism within your heart.

Of course it follows that, in a Traditional society, the Military would carry out the will of the Aristocracy and so would the Economic Caste. The economy would be of minor importance – merely serving the needs of spirituality, culture, land stewardship, politics and defense, unlike today where it is of primary importance. For example, in a healthy society, spirituality and culture are the guiding lights of economics which is the dynamic of absolute politics. But today, economics is the guiding light of spirituality and culture, and politics is no longer absolute; it is reduced to the economics of insider trading. If the economy were treated and respected the way it ought to be, as simply a means of prosperity for the people and not an object of worship or a goal for cultural development, the level of freedom for the Masses would increase ten thousand times compared to what it is today. If people did not value money so highly or covet it so intensely, it would be worth more and would more correctly serve its purpose of providing well-being for all people. But as long as the economy is seen as the most important aspect of society and all choices and goals are weighed against how beneficial or detrimental they will be for the Great and Holy Economy, then there will be poverty, slavery, suffering and lack of freedom. When all is sacrificed on the altar of Mammon, the only one to benefit is Mammon.

How is it that throughout all of human history, the societies that have the least interest in money have the fullest bellies and the most content citizens? All the while, the societies which primarily concern themselves with money and economics have the poorest citizens. Ironic, don't you think?

It is actually quite simple to understand. In the same way that the Ages descend over time, the castes invert over time. In an era of the remote past, humanity had healthy and traditional civilizations with the castes in the proper order: Aristocracy, Military, Economy,

Masses. But similarly to the Golden Age slipping into the Silver, the Military overthrew the wisest people and placed the Aristocracy beneath themselves and militarism was the order of the day. Eventually, the age would descend again and the Economic Caste would overthrow the Military, placing themselves above all others. After some time, the Masses would decide that it is their turn for power and will overthrow the Economic Caste and rule with democracy, communism, barbarism, opinion and preference. When opinions and personal preferences inform policy and politics (a.k.a. democracy), unbiased selfless thinking rooted in objective truth becomes impossible, anarchy reigns, crime is legalized and doom is close at hand. In this condition, the Aristocracy is on the very bottom of the hierarchy, the Culture Bearers are ignored and punished for their unpopular ideas and everything is exactly opposite of the natural spiritual order. This is untenable and something will have to give: either a restoration and realigning of the caste system or a complete collapse of civilization.

This cycle does not completely correspond historically with the grand Descent of the Ages. This cycle occurs at different times in various stages of civilization, sometimes rapidly and sometimes slowly, sometimes in grand ways and other times in subtle ways. An example of one of these inversions is the American and

European Age of Revolution. The Merchant class wanted to overthrow the Aristocracy and convinced the Masses it was for their own good, that is was for democracy. Now the world is ruled by money.

Another example was the Bolshevik Revolution within the Slavic civilization when the purposefully misguided Masses overthrew every caste and attempted to establish total equality and eliminate the impulse toward spirituality. We all know how well that turned out. We can see this pattern starting to take shape in the United States with their firm beliefs in democracy, equality and progress and their obsession with economics. It seems people refuse to learn or to recognize when they are making the same mistakes which already have been made by someone else.

Every great civilization throughout history which has collapsed – which is all of them, by the way – has followed this cycle. Democracy is nothing new. Belief in progress is nothing new. Feminism is nothing new. Voting rights are nothing new. This has all happened a couple dozen times in a couple dozen great civilizations including India, Persia, Egypt, Chaldea, Mesoamerica, China, Greece, Rome, and so on. It has been occurring in our modern civilization for centuries. Ignore this fact at your peril. Your society is not special.

Modern people adore their belief in progress, that our civilization is getting better with time and will be the one that avoids collapse and marches bravely into an infinite future. We are the best and most evolved! All previous civilizations and peoples were failed trials which were simply leading up to us! We have a great destiny! We have all the correct beliefs, the correct ideologies, the correct sciences, the correct laws, the correct governments, the correct cultural and moral values! Our goals are the highest goals! We represent humanity's true interests and ideals! Anyone who disagrees with us is the enemy of humanity itself! We can do no wrong! And the "proof" for this view is the fact that we possess fancier technology, more money and more lenient laws than our ancestors did.

I will give you a helpful little observation: every civilization has believed this about themselves. And yet they have all gone to dust.

The slippery slope of Liberalism – a symptom of descent and decay – has precipitated the destruction of every great civilization that has ever been. After an era of feudalism and strong social cohesion, skepticism and criticism of everything sets in and people wish to be liberated from their obligations to God and His representative the King, then they wish to be liberated from the moral strictures of their communal religion, then they wish to be liberated from their fiscal responsibilities and social contracts to their community, then they wish to be liberated from their responsibilities and roles to their spouses and families, then they wish to be liberated from their gender identities, then they will wish to be liberated from the condition of being a human. Liberalism eventually leads straight to transhumanism[27]. This is the provenance of Ahriman coupled with an unbalanced Luciferic impulse.

This is self-destruction, not progress. This is an urge toward doom fueled by self-hatred and discontentment with reality itself. This is a teenager throwing a temper-tantrum because their parents "just don't get them!" or because "life just isn't fair!" They will throw themselves into drugs, alcohol, partying, hedonism and other libertine individualistic behaviors in an attempt to feel a sense of freedom. It only leads to a temporary sense of euphoria which can allow one to feel like one is in control of their life, but it will actually increase their slavery – slavery to their animal urges, slavery to their emotions, slavery to their thoughts, slavery to their own discontent. Their escapism itself becomes a prison. To the extent a person is enslaved to their own lower instincts and vices is the ease and extent to which they may be enslaved by other people who possess greater will power and cleverness.

Modern industrial civilization and its adherent technologies are an expression of this hedonism mistaken as a step toward freedom and control. Humanity, as it indulges without heed in modern technologies, collectively is like a heroin addict, or a drunken young adult absolutely blacked out on a bender, doing horrible and foolish things to their self, to other people and to the world with a complete lack of self-awareness coupled with a completely undeserved sense of confidence. I will feel sorry for humanity when this collective hangover kicks in. Our children's children will feel such nausea, guilt and shame to such an extent that they will swear off this type of civilization the way an embarrassed and reformed thirty-year-old who misspent their twenties swears off drugs and alcohol.

With every choice you make in your life, especially regarding lifestyle choices, cultural choices, and political choices, ask yourself this one simple question: Will this make my ancestors and descendants proud – what will they think of this choice?

Asking yourself this question as often as you can will build up psychic and spiritual defenses against the temptations and absurdities of the Eighth Sphere, the Superspectrum, and modernity in general.

***

On a large scale, the coherent mass of humanity has been atomized by this so-called "progress" which is in reality an inverting of the proper hierarchy. Extreme individualism has led to there being no individuals in this world – there are only displaced atoms in an ocean of displaced atoms hoping for uniqueness in vain. Fatuous Liberalism has led to there being no liberty in this world – there is only a mutually enforced acceptance of mediocrity and homogeneous thinking. You are free to believe whatever you want, as long as those beliefs are from a limited list of pre-approved options. You are free to do whatever you want, as long as those actions are not proscribed by the tenets of materialism, cosmopolitanism, and the medical tyranny. You are free to live however you want, so long as you have money and pay the racketeer – I mean, tax man.

Many people are beginning to see the Eighth Sphere as an escape from their empty lives and the reprehensible state of modern society. Why deal with what I despise about myself if I can simply alter my physical body with surgery, genetic engineering, pharmaceuticals, and technology? Who needs inner strength, forbearance, and transcendent thinking when I can simply hack off body parts and replace them with things that I prefer? Who needs to balance their inner Divine Masculine and Divine Feminine when they are out of balance if I can just pay for hormone treatments and surgeries to permanently force my body to match my temporarily unbalanced spirit? Why deal with reality if I can enter a virtual computer world with so many pleasures and entertainments?

Ahriman and Lucifer prey on the insecurities and fears of people the way any cult leader, politician, activist, ideologue, demagogue or self-help guru does. Ahriman wants people to believe in his Eighth Sphere. He wants people to live in it. He offers people the cure to what ails them. Is your life boring and meaningless? Just play virtual reality videogames all day. You can be anyone and do anything! Are you lonely? Just use dating apps. Or better yet, here's a virtual boyfriend or girlfriend! You don't need real people when Ahriman's artificial people will never hurt you or say anything that displeases you! Do you miss your deceased parents? Just upload all of your old photos and videos of them and you can produce a virtual replica who will never leave you! Are you sick and tired of being sick and tired? Leave that old meatbag body behind and replace each of your body parts one-by-one, piece-by-piece until you are more machine than man! You will never age or tire!

The yearning for deeper meaning and spiritual immortality will be diverted into hedonism, comfort and sense-enjoyment through the application of technology. People may not notice that paranormal compensations are even occurring around them if their senses are overwhelmed by technological experiences. It is far easier to distract oneself with entertainments and technological conveniences than to practice a spiritual discipline and liberate oneself from suffering that way. When enough people have given themselves over to technology and have turned their backs on spiritual ascent, having cut themselves off from any spiritual experiences including the witnessing of compensation phenomena, Ahriman will have his citizens for his Eighth Sphere kingdom.

This urge for escape will only land them in a new prison of delusions, illusions, electricity, ones and zeroes, doppelgängers and simulacra. Liberalism will lead them not to liberty, but to their final enslavement. They will be enslaved to their lower urges, and they may even be enslaved to Ahriman himself. The constant in-streaming of pleasures and distractions will create a slothful sense of complacency and divert and prevent any urge toward spiritual development. Avoidance of pain results in the failure to gain wisdom. Wisdom comes from pain. So long as this orgy of hedonism, sense-gratification and technology is seen as "progress," humanity is at risk of being lulled into an eternal state of corruption and living death.

However, in the face of all this darkness, ignorance and madness, those who adhere to the spiritual path, unyielding and unceasing, will earn greater triumphs today than any spiritual practitioner throughout all of human history. The most valuable diamonds are formed under the heaviest pressures. The strongest metals are forged in the hottest fires. The most divine spirits have walked through the deepest depths of hell.

Climbing the Tree of Life

As the trunk, branches and leaves of the Cosmic Tree of Life grow and expand, so too do its roots beneath the soil. For everything that takes an ascending step up the Great Tree, something else must be forced downward into the roots to compensate and balance this multi-dimensional reality, otherwise the Tree would become top-heavy and fall over.

This is a hidden cost and the secret war of spiritual advancement. Relating back to the Manvantaras mentioned earlier, when humanity wanted to take on airy bodies and develop higher cognitive faculties, the element of air was placed beneath them. When they wanted to further their cognitive abilities even more and take on watery bodies, the element of water was placed beneath them, and again when humanity took on solid mineral bodies and developed more consciousness and spiritual capability, the mineral kingdom was placed beneath them. Something must be forced down into matter below that entity which is ascending in spirit.

Humanity is utilizing the mineral kingdom in very sophisticated ways. From smelting iron to forge hand tools to burning coal in order to create steam and generate electricity to finding novel combinations of minerals such as silicon, copper, gold, iron, zinc, and so on, to create microchips. We have built interesting technologies that carry out tasks and perform labor. We have named these machines calculators, computers, programs, and oddly enough, demons. The programs that run in the background of your computer which carry out the most basic and fundamental processes which allow you to use one of these devices have been dubbed "demons" by the computer scientists who created them.

When one examines a single silicon wafer microchip circuit that has been inlaid on its little green circuit board, it bears a remarkable resemblance to the layout of the fabled Temple of Solomon, which was said to have been built by demons which were enslaved by Solomon.

This toponymy makes one wonder what these computer scientists were thinking when naming their mysterious little programs. Are they involved with the group of people who desire to build the so-called Third Temple which is prophesied to be the throne of God on Earth? Is computer infrastructure the temple itself? If so, is this "God" of theirs merely some sort of computer program like an artificial intelligence which will use our networked digital devices as its throne?

But it is my opinion that intelligence cannot be artificial. There is a very popular school of thought that consciousness is created by the brain – that matter comes together in such a way as to create the brain and produce the phenomenon that we call consciousness. I do not see how something higher (consciousness) can be produced by something lower (matter.) This seems a logical fallacy. Also, it flies in the face of even the most basic of rules in materialistic science: the product of a reaction must exist somewhere within the reagents. This means that if consciousness is produced by the brain, then consciousness itself must be part of that which created the brain.

Another theory is that the brain and the body are more like an antenna which receives consciousness from another source. The way a remote-control sends radio waves to a toy car and produces activity in the toy, so do our brain and heart receive the "radio waves" of consciousness which produces activity in our body and mind.

I really do not think that someone can mash some silicon and other minerals together and create consciousness. However, they can probably create a type of electro-mechanical brain that can house or receive a pre-existing consciousness.

John Keel's "Trojan Horse" comes to mind. Perhaps somewhere just beyond sight, Ahriman awaits the day that his minions within humanity finish building his brain and body – his temple – so that he may take possession of it and interact more intimately with our world. He may even convince many that he is in fact God.

The famous proponent of transhumanism, Ray Kurzweil, when asked whether he thinks God exists, replied, "Not yet[28]." He believes that humanity will eventually invent God through the application of computer technology. He also believes that one day, engineers will be able to create immortal versions of deceased people by digitizing as much of a person's history as possible: photographs, videos, audio recordings, journal entries, work life, interviews and questionnaires about the person, and so on. In this way, a virtual person can be created and animated in some sort of computer environment that may be interacted with, and this digital doppelgänger will respond to the user's interactions in ways that are theoretically accurate to how the person would react if they were still alive. This idea came to Kurzweil after his father died and he was distraught to the point of desperation with this loss. He is a textbook example of the "traumatized scientist" described by Michael Barnes in the *Encyclopedia of Trauma*[29]. This is a person who is unable to spiritually or psychologically heal from trauma and considers the event that led to their trauma to be an inherently unfair problem that must be solved through the application of science. This is the type of person who refuses to do inner work and instead attempts to alter the outside world until it feels safe and satisfactory for them. In Kurzweil's case, he believes death is a disease that must be cured so that he will not suffer loss ever again. In my opinion, this is a frightening form of delusion and in many fictional stories, the traumatized scientist is a common archetype for the main villain – relatable and sympathetic certainly, but extremely deluded and dangerous.

He is not alone in his views. Many transhumanists and technology enthusiasts subscribe to their own materialistic religion which contains its own messianic prophecies. The same way that Christians believe that the Second Coming of Christ will solve all problems, cure all diseases, relieve all woes, and provide immortality for the chosen ones, the transhumanists believe in the same exact thing, but instead of considering this event to be the return of a God-Man, they call it The Singularity. It is based on Moore's Law, also known as the Exponential Primer or the Law of Accelerating Returns.

In the mid Twentieth Century, Gordon Moore noticed that the number of transistors contained in an integrated microchip doubles every two years. Some computer engineers took this idea and predicted that this would continue to occur until there would be an infinite number of electrical components on an infinitely small electronic device that would reproduce itself an infinite amount of times on an infinitely short time scale. It is said by technology enthusiasts, that on this day, the ultimate super computer will come into existence and the Machine God will awaken. It will solve all of the universe's problems, all diseases will be cured, humanity will be given technological and genetic modifications that will render them immortal and all-knowing, and all mysteries of the cosmos and the science of governance will be revealed thus creating the perfect society and transforming the very fabric of reality. It is essentially a messianic religion for atheists.

I would like to point out the obvious: this should be called "Moore's Hypothesis" – not "law" – considering the fact that this Singularity has not yet happened; there is no conclusive evidence that there will continue to be exponential increases in technological advancements. Even Gordon Moore himself modified his observation in 1975 and concluded that the returns were in fact beginning to diminish. The Exponential Primer is nothing more than a prediction, and predictions cannot, by definition, be considered scientific laws. The fact that this misnomer stands to this day and that it has so many millions of fanatical adherents, some of whom plan and schedule the growth of their technology corporations based on this time-scale, tells me that this concept is a dogmatic tenet of a religious cult.

Singularity theorists at first believed that their great messianic moment might occur in the 1980's, but when the decade came and went, they kept pushing the date back, first into the 1990's then into the early 2000's. Today, they are holding onto the date of 2045. It reminds me of priests who would schedule the building of churches, the coronations of kings, the ordainment of bishops and other preparations for the return of the Messiah in accordance with the Millennial predictions that the Eschaton would occur at the New Year 1000_{AD} or again in 1666_{AD} or again in 1998_{AD} or again in 2000_{AD} or again in 2012_{AD} yet here we remain. All these dates came and went.

Simply because one subscribes to materialism, atheism and modern science does not mean that their predictions are any more sound than your average hobo prophet wearing an old pizza box around his neck with the words "The End is Nigh" painted upon it. It is a rare person indeed who is immune to wishful thinking, dogma, and fanaticism. No matter how sober a materialist may appear, the belief in modern science inculcates within the mind of the believer an entire plethora of superstitions and biases that are not regarded as such out of arrogance, pride, lack of self-awareness and a general ignorance of history, philosophy and the desperate desire for saviors that arises within the hearts of a population during the collapsing stage of any given civilization. Attempt an argument with a materialist who wholeheartedly believes in the tenets of modern science and you will see a calm and self-assured scholar degenerate into a barking rabid dog, positively incensed and enraged at your audacity to question the great modern church of science. Watch how this allegedly objective personality resorts to *ad homonym* attacks against you and attempts to not only take the moral high ground, but invent it out of thin air as morality has no place in a discussion about knowledge, but since their knowledge is lacking and impotent, they result to moralisms in order to win a debate. They will attempt to turn the tables and persuade you that believing in science is somehow more moral than holding other beliefs; like a Catholic who claims that their church has helped more people than any other institution in human history, a believer in science will claim the same about their institutions. The debate quickly becomes asinine, directionless, emotional and vapid. This style of debating which was adopted by Catholic clergy in the medieval era is now used by modern scientists to the same ends: to prove that they deserve all the political power and wealth available in society and to belittle and embarrass their opponents with fear and guilt.

Again, this sort of fanaticism and dogma

brings Ahriman great joy, as these types of personalities work to bring Ahriman's goals into fruition whether they realize it or not. Make no mistake, many of the ideals of The Enlightenment era have been crystallized into the doctrine of materialism which has led directly to the religion of transhumanism. With all of this in play, and the heavy emotional baggage associated with it, humanity runs the risk of severing their selves from their spiritual heritage by enveloping themselves in materialism and technology.

***

And envelope they shall. The transhumanists believe that they may climb the Tree of Life through the application of technology. Instead of developing telepathy, they will use telecommunications devices. Instead of developing spiritual sight, they will use meters and readers calibrated with quartz crystal and golden antennae. Instead of developing their throat chakra and communication skills, they will use computer programs that use predictive dictation models. Instead of developing logic, they will use calculators and simulators. Instead of astral traveling, they will lose themselves in virtual reality games and experiences. Instead of opening their root chakra and communing with their ancestors, they will interact with digital simulacra of their forebears. Instead of working on their solar plexus chakra, they will seek personal power through the ingestion of pharmaceuticals. Instead of working with the sacral chakra and developing loving sexual relationships, they will expend their energies through pornography. Instead of working on their heart chakra and emotional issues, they will modulate their emotions with designer drugs.

Utilizing the mineral, plant and animal kingdoms (all of which are lower than the human kingdom), they attempt to move upward in this reality. Industrial civilization and computer science stems from the manipulation of minerals. Pharmacology stems from the manipulation of plants and minerals. Genetic modification stems from the manipulation of animals and plants. When an engineer combines various minerals like quartz crystal, silicon, and gold and creates a cell phone, his power remains unchanged. He is still the same human he was before. When he uses that phone to talk to another person, only the phones are connecting to each other. The connection of the people through the phone is incidental and tangential. The spiritual, mental and physical faculties of the people remain unchanged. However, the mineral kingdom has just been developed further and higher than it was before. What was once a lump of minerals is now a computer processor. The human engineer was used as a womb to birth into existence a higher development for the minerals used in the construction of a novel piece of technology, much in the same way that beings higher than the human kingdom have aided in the creation and evolution of humans. This is simultaneously beautiful, creative, hopeful and astonishingly dangerous and detrimental if mishandled.

When transhumanists say that computers make people smarter, this is nonsense. Plato warned that the use of the written word and the proliferation of books would render memory obsolete. He feared people would become forgetful if they no longer needed to exercise the faculty of memory; like an unused muscle, it would atrophy, weaken, and potentially die. Think how much more this applies to today's situation when considering all of the tasks and faculties that modern technologists wish to take away from humans and put into the hands of machines for the sake of convenience, power and luxury.

A more correct statement would be that computers have made the mineral kingdom smarter and humans have remained the same. Some people have certainly improved their well-being with computers, others have diminished their well-being (to say the least.) On the average, not much has changed with the human being itself, but a great deal has changed for the mineral kingdom. It is evolving while humanity is stagnating. Follow this thought experiment further and we may see humanity's throne in this world usurped by a pretender.

The mythological cycle can be alluded to here: the titans who created the gods were overthrown by the gods. In modern mythology, particularly in sci-fi and fantasy stories, the gods who created humans are overthrown by humans. Perhaps in the future the humans who have created machines will be overthrown by machines. I wonder who the machines will create and be overthrown by? Little Grays perhaps?

I am also reminded of the many accounts and legends of people who have built golems. We have such famous stories as *The Golem of Prague, Frankenstein,* and *Fantasia*. A magician will create a man-shaped object out of clay or wood or dead material and will perform a ritual or process which breathes life into it. He then commands this entity to perform some menial and utilitarian tasks, but he fails to give limited and explicit instructions and this results in catastrophe. For example, Mickey Mouse tells his army of sentient broom sticks to fill a basin with water. Well, they certainly do this. But Mickey never told them when to stop, so they kept filling the basin beyond its limit and he flooded the entire building. Nick Bostrom warns of this regarding the creation of artificial general intelligence in his book, *Superintelligence*[30]. He mentions that if we create an intelligent machine and program it to make paperclips, it may go on making paper clips until it has converted all of the matter in the solar system into quadrillions of paperclips. Or if we program it to make humans happy, it may go around implanting electrodes into all of our bodies stimulating the parts of our brains that are active during moments of happiness, or stimulating our face muscles so that we are always smiling. We may be creating far more harm than good in our blind and fast-paced desire to build advanced computer systems.

Ascending the Tree of Life seems to have a brutal aspect to it. When the titans ascended, they created the gods to push beneath themselves. When the gods ascended, they created humans to push beneath themselves. Will humans need to create sentient machines to push beneath ourselves in order to ascend? Is this necessary and inevitable? Can it or should it be avoided? If we avoid it, will we be robbing a potential life-form of its chance at life – like aborting a fetus? It seems that all of these newly created beings eventually assert their own freedom despite their creators anyway. What is the correct course of action? This is a deep and serious question on which we all must reflect.

Rudolf Steiner mentioned after one of his clairvoyant reveries that everything, every machine, that we create for beauty and creativity will add to the good of the future, and everything, every machine, we create to satisfy utilitarian desires will add to the evil of the future. He even mentioned that the machines which we use for utility will eventually rise up and wage war against us in the distant future. He mentioned this in 1908, long before *The Terminator* or *The Matrix* were released in theaters. Even filmmaker Fritz Lang seemed cognizant of this threat portrayed in his *Metropolis* (1927.)

Keep this in mind when using modern technology. When you are on your computer or your phone, ask yourself whether or not you need to be using it. What are you doing? Are you satisfying some sense of boredom? Are you creating a work of art? Are you paying your bills? Are you learning something? What exactly is the intent and purpose of your time using this machine? I am not putting a moral judgment on anything, I am only asking you to be self-aware and totally conscious during your time on the computer. Simply remember yourself – remember where you are, who you are, and what you are doing and why you are doing it. Do not lose yourself in this experience. Observe it and rise above it. Moderate and control your interactions with technology and do not allow them to dominate your mind or your feelings. Take a step back if you feel yourself becoming lost, hypnotized or entranced by scrolling through social media. Take a step back if you feel yourself becoming agitated by some news article or video posted by some talking head. Make sure that you have a clear and focused purpose for using your computer or phone and when that goal is achieved, go do something else.

Developing Discernment

Tricksters abound! This world is full of them. Tricksters depend on one thing more than any other: ignorance. It is their sharpest tool, their most effective weapon, and they will use it against you every chance they get. Magicians, of course, never reveal their tricks. They must maintain ignorance within society at large in order to insure their career. Sometimes they use deception to gain power over you, to take something from you, or just for shits and giggles. Sometimes tricksters may even use deception in a benevolent manner to dispel ignorance and cure you of it – to grant knowledge; a sort of "tough love" wake up call, or a harshly precocious way of holding up a mirror to you, pushing you to your limit and forcing you to face your own ignorance or to face an issue which you have been neglecting.

Tricksters can be humans, animals, entities from the Superspectrum, or even your own perceptions, thoughts and feelings.

The latter, in most cases, stems from misunderstandings or mistakes and not from malicious intent – although occasionally one's inner voice can be quite cruel, in which case, I advise you do something about that, seek healing, and do not let it continue. I am sure you have enough people trying to pull a fast one on you in this life; you should not be doing it to yourself.

Tricksters in the animal kingdom are as deadly as they are hilarious, and they are always fascinating. Spiders, foxes, coyotes, copperheads, chameleons, and other camouflaged critters are experts at laying traps and luring unsuspecting prey into their clutches. They deceive the senses by producing sights, sounds and smells that are simulacra of the real things. A copperhead snake produces the smell of a cucumber to lure furry forest frolickers into their dining room. Coyotes can throw their voices like ventriloquists and produce the illusion that they are far away in one direction, causing their prey to turn and run in the opposite direction where they lay in ambush.

The human kingdom has taken the talents of deception and trickery to far greater levels. We have everything from filmmakers and stage magicians to intelligence officers and military strategists to serial killers and wet workers using unimaginable skills and technologies and mobilizing vast resources to produce illusions that not only amaze and entertain crowds of onlookers, but can lure targets to their doom, turn the tides of war, or even shape the minds and opinions of entire populations. You do not possess media literacy or an understanding of propaganda and governance until you have come to understand the tools of trickery and deception, both modern and ancient, technological and occult.

Even after only a cursory study of the tools of this trade, you should begin questioning the commonly held theories about the origins of various paranormal phenomena. These theories are generally as follows: spirits of dead people, aliens and spaceships from other planets, denizens of underground super-civilizations, demons, angels, fairies, spirit guides, schizophrenia, multiple personality disorder, figments of imagination, or improperly identified mundane phenomena. These are all plausible and can be sensible or even true in certain scenarios, but they are a bit old and tired and do not explain the overwhelming majority of authentic paranormal encounters. If they did, that would mean alien spaceships are landing approximately three million times per year on this planet. I highly doubt that is occurring. The study of paranormal phenomena has stagnated over the last sixty years. Researchers have become attached to these prevailing theories and their ideas have become ossified and their perspectives limited. In some circles, questioning the Extraterrestrial Hypothesis is equivalent to blaspheming within a church. In New Age groups, if you question the veracity of the spirit guides, you may as well be trying to convince an astrophysicist that the world is flat.

Very rarely will someone say that the goofy robots you saw which wobbled out of a parked spaceship were produced by a hypnotic ritual performed by an occultist sitting in a cave in Mongolia. It is not likely that someone will explain your horrifying medical examination by Little Gray aliens and preying mantis people as being caused by a handful of operatives from the Office of Naval Intelligence. When you experience a euphoric spiritual contact with an angelic blonde man from the Pleiades who reveals to you all of the mysteries of reality, would you be shocked to learn you had been zapped by a handheld microwave gun that stimulated certain parts of your brain and the experience was orchestrated by some dude in a van parked across the street? Or better yet, the microwave beam was emitted by a satellite in orbit around the earth – no creepy van necessary. When killers report that they heard a voice in their head that tormented them until they carried out its sadistic orders, would you be surprised to learn that this devil-on-the-shoulder was in fact an officer of the Central Intelligence Agency? Or more bizarre yet, maybe it really was the devil.

Sci-fi author Philip K. Dick considered some of these theories throughout his life after his intense paranormal contacts. He entertained the possibility that the Soviets or the FBI were messing with him for political and social engineering purposes. At other times, he believed he was being deceived by a demon or manipulated by an ancient supercomputer. Then he thought that the soul of an enlightened Greek saint from long ago was invading his consciousness and giving him spiritual knowledge. He settled on the theory that it was Christ Himself providing him with a great spiritual awakening and purifying his mind and even altering and correcting the past in order to produce a better future – an eery analog to contemporary theories about the Mandela Effect and CERN's Large Hadron Collider. Most prophets, ancient and modern, who have these experiences generally have no idea what the hell happened to them or if they could trust the memory of it, and they spend the rest of their lives trying to make sense of it.

This is why I am highly skeptical of trance-channelers, psychic mediums, near death experiencers and people who have had sudden catastrophic spiritual awakenings who are so certain that they have been chosen by the Higher Powers to spread a message of light and love and their only test against their experience to determine if it is true or not is to remember if the channeling or event felt good or if it felt bad. If it feels loving and pleasant, it is the truth, and if it feels "negative" and unpleasant, it is false. In my opinion, this is an absurd metric for veracity. (Thankfully many mediums these days are becoming far more skilled, self-aware and discerning.) Speaking from experience, I have been at the center of my fair share of paranormal phenomena, and let me tell you, it is anything but straightforward. Anyone who is certain of its origins is either extremely wise and spiritually advanced to possess such certainty and clarity, or they are naive to the grossest degree and simply *want* to believe whatever it is they experienced at face value. Consider people like Helena Blavatsky, Annie Besant, Helena Roerich, Alice Bailey and the like. These people, as well-meaning and kindhearted as they may have been, were among the most easily deceived arrogant egoists this world has ever seen. Many natural-born sensitives believe that they do not need to improve their intellects or study anything intently because they readily receive messages of pure knowledge from higher beings. They feel they have a direct connection to the truth and do not need to discern whether or not it is in fact truthful. They feel that they do not need to support it with research, book learning, life experience, experimentation, second opinions or discrimination. They simply assume that it is the truth. Why shouldn't it be? They were chosen because they are special. End of doubt.

These personalities wanted so badly to believe that they were great inaugurators of a new civilization, a New Age; that they were chosen by the Ascended Masters; that they were holy and special in some way – even to the extent that one of them was so certain of their important mission and moral high ground that they exploited an eleven-year-old boy for seven years grooming him to be some kind of messianic figure, a World Teacher. This poor boy lost his childhood and very nearly his mind because of the delusions of some New Age prophetess. (Thankfully the eighteen-year-old Jiddu Krishnarmurti broke free from this borderline abusive relationship and, in fact, went on to become a great spiritual teacher in his own right, however; he taught things with which the Theosophical Society – the cult from which he extricated himself – vehemently disagreed.)

And perhaps these people were great inaugurators of a New Age. Perhaps they have done far more good than harm. I sincerely hope that is the case. But we must not put such personalities on a pedestal. At the end of the day, whether one is a pauper, a politician, a professor, a pontiff, a priest, a prophet, or a psychic (did you pronounce it with a "P?"), the human mind essentially works the same way in all of us and we are all subject to foolishness, mistakes, misinterpretations, misrepresentations and deceptions.

Now I am not trying to make you look over your shoulder or sow the seeds of doubt regarding any transformative spiritual experiences you may have had in your life or to doubt any and all mediums and psychics. I am also not suggesting that you close yourself off from the higher spiritual currents out of fear of tricksters or demons. Seek wisdom and peace in the ways which work for you and serve your highest potential. You may judge a tree by the fruit it bears! You must decide for yourself the degrees to which you will follow the path of reason and the path of revelation. Every ardent seeker finds the ratio that works for them eventually.

And if you are considering the path of revelation and feel like slipping into a short bout of paranoia, do some quick research on the so-called "voice to skull" (or V2K) technology. You will never look at windowless vans the same way again. Or peruse the thousands of files declassified in 2017 of *Project Stargate*[31]. Or perhaps you have heard of a little program called MKULTRA. I am sure you will find something that tickles your fancy which you can use to start a conversation at your next family dinner.

***

Building discernment regarding the origins of paranormal phenomena begins by understanding perception itself. Before you try to figure out where that UFO came from or how that ghost walked into your living room, you should first understand how your sense-organs work and how percepts are formed in your consciousness.

Honestly, you should do this before you even try to study how trees grow from acorns. Many people skip this step for many reasons. It is so obvious and close to us that it often goes overlooked. Once it is noticed, the person realizes that it is not so easy to understand these fundamental aspects of ourselves. It can take lifetimes of spiritual discipline, self-awareness training, experience and inner searching. And so they persuade themselves that it is simply not that important and carry on with their external researches anyway. But, I am sorry to break it to you, failing in this discipline will result in a failure to understand psychic and paranormal phenomena, even mundane phenomena. You will fail before you even begin. Plain and simple. In fact, tricksters depend on the likelihood that you will fail in this. They constantly exploit this weakness. It is of great benefit to tricksters that modern researchers and scientists do not have any type of consciousness training regimen integrated into their lifestyles. Most of them are not even aware that they require such training. This is to the detriment of us all.

A stark wake up call for me regarding the functioning of my senses occurred when I was a teenager and took psilocybin mushrooms for the first time. (I have always been an experimental psychonaut, but stopped ingesting entheogens when I was eighteen years old. I do not condone or recommend the use of hallucinogens or any other drugs except under the supervision of a qualified doctor, a sane and healthy confidante or trusted shaman, even then, a healthy and well-adjusted person should not need to do this. It is for therapeutic purposes and should not be used recreationally.) This is known as the Corrosive Path to alchemists – the ingestion of drugs in an attempt to alter the mind to perceive more of reality – to corrode the limitations placed on their consciousness. It is characterized by a desire for a shortcut to mystical experience or a hopeless feeling that without these pharmaceutical aides the alchemist will never gain the Beatific Vision. But it is known as "corrosive" for a reason: it may dissolve one's personality and sanity. Of course it may restore sanity and health in an unwell person under proper therapeutic guidance. But again, a healthy and sane person puts their mind at risk when ingesting these substances.

Many modern people, especially among hippies, neo-pagans and technologists, swear by the use of hallucinogens. (There is in fact enormous cross-over between the counter-culture movement of the 60's and 70's and the industry of computer science. Modern computer science was largely born from drug-using counter-culturalists.) They love to rant and rave about the health benefits and the transcendent spiritual knowledge that they have gained and so on and so forth. That has not been my experience. To me, it was not an upward movement of consciousness, but a lateral movement. I can easily see why it is commonly mistaken for an upward movement. It may have allowed me to see more of reality, but it was mostly illusory and it felt atavistic, like a memory from some bygone moon-brained period of an earlier era in the human timeline when we could not tell where the mountaintop ended and the sky began. It sometimes also just felt like the mushrooms were attempting to communicate with me and I was simply experiencing a type of fungal consciousness communion within my human mind. A novel and charming experience, to be sure, but not exactly a spiritual awakening. I suppose I am just not that easily impressed.

What I did learn, however, was extremely valuable. I learned that not only my perceptions, but my identity, sense of self and even my entire world can utterly transform and change into something completely different and alien with just a minor change to my body's chemistry. All I needed to do was put a small mushroom on my peanut butter sandwich and within an hour I was a six-armed pin wheel of energy and light surfing around an undulating alien planet of impossible shapes, sounds, colors and creatures.

I have never trusted my sense organs since. Your central nervous system can be manipulated so easily and produce not only minor hallucinations and voices in your head, but entirely new identities, worlds, and experiences of reality. If a tiny amount of fungus can do that, what about all of the radiation from space with which we are constantly bombarded? What about all of the electromagnetic pollution from our telecommunications infrastructure? What about all the foods we eat on a regular basis – natural or processed? How do all of these things affect our perceptions? Even if we had the most pure, isolated nervous system, how can we be sure that it provides us with an accurate representation of reality? How do we know that we are all not constantly hallucinating a collective dream of illusions?

There is no way to prove whether reality is real. You cannot say whether this world is real or illusion. It is simply impossible. At least as long as you view this reality from the human perspective. We have no frame of reference. Your body, your sense organs, your mind and your consciousness are not equipped to understand reality. They are equipped to play the game of human life on the surface of a seemingly solid planet, but that is about all they are good for. Think about an amoeba in a petri dish in a laboratory. What the hell do they know about petri dishes or microscopes or the biological sciences? They are equipped to swim around and multiply and not much else. They will never know anything about being an amoeba or do anything else until they stop existing as amoebae and begin existing as a higher form of life. It is the biologist who understands the amoeba. The amoeba does not understand itself.

This is the same for human beings. The only way to understand what it is to be human is to be something other than – higher than – human. To be suprahuman is the goal of spiritual discipline, of initiation, and this is the only way in which discernment can be developed. Anything short of this is too little to understand your perceptions and experiences, whether sober, under the influence of entheogens, or experiencing a paranormal phenomenon. Gaining the higher perspective is the first and last job of gaining understanding. A tree cannot perceive the forest, but the Sun illuminates all. Stop being the tree and be the Sun instead.

How can a person cross that infinite gulf between humanity and suprahumanity? The same way an acorn crosses the infinite gulf between acornity and treedom – with proper nourishment. If you break open a seed, you will find that it is in fact empty. How can this empty shell contain within itself the knowledge, energy and blueprints for growing into a full-fledged plant replete with stalks, branches, flowers, and fruit? It seems impossible. It is so strange and mysterious and miraculous. It is buried in fertile soil, given some water and sunlight, and the rest happens on its own. How bizarre. When a human examines their self and asks the question: How can I be more than what I am now? the same sense of impossibility may overwhelm the questioner. And when looking within oneself, one ultimately finds only emptiness. But if that tiny empty shell contains the power to grow into a tree, surely you contain the power to grow into a suprahuman. Does the acorn ask: How do I become a mighty oak? No. It just does it.

Perhaps this is where the analogy falls apart. A person is not an acorn. We are burdened with choices, actions, will, emotions, thoughts, and so on. We must take a great deal of our development into our own hands and walk the proper paths in life. However, some of these choices are as simple as allowing ourselves to be buried in fertile soil and shower ourselves with fresh water and sunlight. We must place ourselves in environments which are conducive to personal spiritual growth. This does not mean hiding away in a monastery, living in a well-provided cozy home, being surrounded only by positive reinforcement, and transforming our outer world into some kind of safe space full of zen gardens, patchouli incense, mantra chanting, and guided meditations. Although if that is what you are into and have the privilege to live like that, I say go for it. But most of us will be stuck at boring jobs, with difficult families, annoying friends, demanding co-workers, bills to pay, and spouses to support and live alongside.

But perhaps this is the fertile soil, water and sunlight necessary for your growth. These difficulties, mundanities and trials may be just what you need to develop your spiritual faculties. When you live in a luxurious home full of crystal singing bowls and videos playing in the background all day of pretty girls repeating positive affirmations, you might find yourself becoming extraordinarily weak, like muscles gone unused. Sometimes you need to spend all week tack-welding hundreds of steel joints in an industrial factory to learn how to single-pointedly focus your mind. Sometimes you need to wash the dirty dishes that your wife and her friends carelessly left in the sink to learn where your emotional triggers are within yourself. Sometimes you need to be overworked, miss a deadline and be yelled at by your insufferable boss to learn what really matters in life, what to prioritize, what to give minimal effort and how to let things roll off of you like water off a duck's back. Submerging yourself in everyday modern life may be one of the highest forms of initiation ever offered to a human being throughout all of our history. Those who run for the hills – literally – into their monasteries with the other disaffected monks or into luxury condos in New Mexico or Bali with all the other crystal-gripping influencers are missing out on one of history's greatest opportunities: the opportunity to suffer gracefully like a real human being, down in the dirt with everyone else.

If you can suffer this life and still manage to dig deep within yourself and choose to feel happiness and spread that joy regardless of your outer circumstances, you will be most favored of God. Happiness is indeed a choice to be made, a skill to be practiced and mastered, a muscle to be exercised. It gets easier and easier to be happy the more you choose to feel it and exercise it. From that center of happiness and serenity in your heart, it becomes easier and easier to make ethical choices regarding yourself, others, and the world, which is, after all, the great task of initiation we have before us. All it takes is self-remembrance. Whenever you do something, just remember yourself. Here I am whisking some pancake batter in my kitchen. Here I am sitting in a chair reading my work reports. Here I am playing with my children. Here I am scrubbing my back in the shower. I feel the water running over me, I am aware of the temperature, the sensation, the weight of my body on my feet and knees, the thoughts flitting through my mind. Oh, here comes an emotion and there it goes. Step back and notice. Observe yourself as often as you can. The more you remember to observe yourself, the more you become self-aware. The more self-aware you become, the more self-controlled you are. The more self-controlled you are, the more you can choose which emotions to feel and which ones to eliminate and sublimate. When you regulate your emotions, you unlock your ability to advance automatically on the spiritual path like a plant receiving water and sunlight.

With the near-total loss of The Tradition and its public institutions, the festivals of awakening and the trials of initiation, we have been given an excellent replacement: everyday modern life. Your attitude toward this life will determine whether you are just another miserable soul-dead automaton going about your routine or if you are a spiritual warrior advancing through the degrees of awakening. Outwardly, you both look the same and perform the same activities, but inwardly one is soaring to infinite heights and gaining immeasurable power. It is only a matter of perspective and the application of the Golden Rule.

This is the bulk of the work. As you suffer gracefully and exercise your whole being, your spiritual faculties develop, your intellect and discernment become more acute and accurate. Your intuition will speak more truthfully and loudly to you. You will find yourself in various situations and your heart will give you sound advice that when followed, leads to goodness in your life and the lives of those around you. This is how you will begin to tell truth from falsehood. It is difficult to put into words because it is rooted in a transcendent sphere higher than concept and language. But it works like water and sunshine on a seed. It just works. The seed does not know how or why it grows into a tree, and neither do you. But you do not need to understand it in order for it to happen.

And the good thing is, you do not need me, some old book, a Pleiadean space brother, or some spirit guide channeled through the larynx of a wine drinking soccer mom who read *The Celestine Prophecy* fourteen times to tell you this. It is a simple and common-sense application of something which five minutes of inner searching will reveal to you.

So be glad that this dark age offers such a brilliant way to develop discernment and our other spiritual faculties. Pain and monotony become wisdom as long as you are consistently conscious of yourself. Everyday life becomes the initiation. As the Zen Buddhists say, "Shut up and carry water" (or something to that effect.)

Interaction with Technology and the Stratification of Society

Humans like to use their opposable thumbs and clever minds to interact with their environment. This has allowed us to create with beauty and practicality, art and science. When art and science come together and merge, we get technology. The science of understanding that a sharp thing can cut through a soft thing and the art of deftly chipping away at a stone to create an edge has led to the development of hatchets and knives. This intersection of science and art carries through the heart of all of humanity's technological endeavors and innovations.

Today, it is common practice that anthropologists, archaeologists, evolutionary theorists, psychologists and other researchers examine the development of tools and technology from its earliest known appearance in our world and formulate opinions on what they see. This has divided researchers, theorists and technologists into different schools of thought regarding how humanity interacts with their environment and with the tools we create. We have naturalists, Luddites, cyberneticists, transhumanists, Burkean conservatives, Mennonites, industrialists, futurists, primitivists, nihilists, accelerationists, humanists, Butlerians, Neo-Platonists, and so on and such like. There are as many opinions about technology as there are people in the world.

There are extremists in these schools of thought with unbalanced ideas about technology. There are primitivists on one end of the spectrum and transhumanists on the other. Having extremists in the world is a fact of life; there is not much we can do about that. For the most part, it is alright for them to exist as long as their ideology and extremism is obvious to everyone. For example, not many people will take primitivists seriously. Most of us understand that no matter how much we may dislike technology, it likely is not going anywhere any time soon. Technology is here, we use it, we adapt to its use and we expand upon its innovations and we try to do our best not to use the technologies which we dislike. The genie is out of the bottle, so to speak. When a primitivist begins a discourse (or more likely a rant) about the superiority of primitive life, their words fall mostly on deaf ears due to the fact that living a primitive life today is essentially impossible and far more trouble than it is worth. The impulse of primitivism is reactionary at best and destructive at worst. This is clear and obvious to most people and we leave these extremists to their little groups to plot the overthrow of industrial civilization, write their manifestos about how much they hate airplanes, or to build some Neolithic-style commune. They are more of a nuisance than a threat and their ideology will likely never take root in our social consciousness.

However, on the other end of the spectrum, this next group of extremists are not recognized as extremists. They are seen by many as futurists and innovators, as brave and ingenious "disruptors" of the status quo. They offer promises of power, wealth, happiness, health and a brighter future for humanity in general. Since the 1990's, transhumanists have been given a spotlight. They have written and published countless best selling books. They have been interviewed on the most popular and prestigious journalistic programs and have been given softball questions and the weakest challenges to their beliefs by these so-called "professional" journalists allowing them to proselytize to their hearts' content. The media and academia have given them a veritable soapbox to stand on, nay, a pulpit from which to preach their Good News to the gentiles begging for enlightenment and salvation. (Thankfully modern academia is no longer as monolithic as it once was. There is currently healthy and much-needed push-back coming from bio-ethics councils and technological outcomes think tanks.)

Transhumanists boldly discuss their theories as if they are facts. They attempt to predict the future as if they are visionary prophets who have understood the portents of the times. They are so certain of the beneficial, near Utopian, future outcomes of the application of new discoveries in biomedical technologies, computer science, pharmacology, and genetic science, even though many of these technologies and their uses are still entirely theoretical or have only seen limited success, or even outright failure, in small clinical and experimental applications. They are like a radical priesthood of a new cult attempting to swell their ranks through missionary preaching and conversion. They believe that striving toward transhumanism is the most natural and basic urge that humanity possesses and they will attempt to convince you that everyone is a transhumanist in their heart of hearts according to human nature itself. To some, it is even considered a moral imperative to support transhumanists in their ventures to alleviate human suffering and expand human capability.

I have heard the argument that if you use even so much as a rock to smash open an oyster, you are a transhumanist (or maybe even a trans-otterist.) You have used a technology to augment your abilities, you have merged with a thing outside of yourself to accomplish a task with ease that would have otherwise been very difficult with your own hands and faculties. A rock turned into a flint axe which turned into a pulley system which turned into a steel hammer which turned into industrial machinery which turned into computers, and so on. Therefore, genetic alterations, pharmaceutical preparations, mechanical body modifications and digital brain-computer augmentations are perfectly normal and follow naturally from your use of a rock to smash an oyster.

It is my opinion that this is an absurd hyperbole. The word "exaggeration" is not strong enough to describe this bizarre argument. It is the same tactic used by stage magicians and fraudulent psychics: they fill your mind with alien notions that do not belong to you but use linguistic, logical and charismatic trickery to make these ideas seem perfectly natural and as though you believed these things all along. Then they perform their spectacular trick after you have been conditioned with a false expectation. You are then much more likely to be deceived and believe in them, to be impressed with them and even thank them for the experience.

If you believe that using a rock, an axe, or a shovel is the equivalent of putting microchips in your brain or lopping off body parts and replacing them with machinery or taking hormone or genetic treatments to positively select alterations to your body, then you and I have drawn the line between tool usage and transhumanism in very different places.

**

Transhumanists may discover that they will have severe issues with phantom limb syndrome and metabolic issues once they begin replacing or adding body parts.

The human being is not only a physical body as transhumanists religiously believe. They consider their self to be nothing more than a collection of minerals and goo, so there should not be any harm in replacing minerals and goo with different types of minerals and goo. They will be in for a shock once they discover that the human being is also composed of an ether body, an astral body, a mind, and a spirit.

There is a facetious question which I enjoy asking materialists, especially biologists and others who hold doctorates in the medical field. What is life? Biology is the study of life, you hold a doctorate in biology, a.k.a. life study. What is life? My body is composed of carbon, calcium, iron, zinc, etc. etc. and so is that cold corpse in the morgue over there. Why am I warm and breathing and he is not? Why is my heart beating and his has stopped? Why am I thinking and perceiving while he does not? Why can I will my body to move, yet he cannot? What is the difference between me and that corpse?

To this date, I must have asked this to about twenty or twenty five doctors and I have received only one considered answer from a spiritually inclined physician. All the others have either scoffed or laughed or accused me of ignorance, of not being initiated into their great science, or they came up with some off-the-cuff hare-brained theory that sounds more like they were attempting to convince themselves than to convince me.

Just a single session of training in the occult Tradition or even an hour of Chigong would set these doctors on a path of discovery and knowledge. It really is not that difficult to discover and sense your own etheric body. Human beings have trained each other to do this for many thousands of years with predictable, replicated results. But they usually never take that first step. It generally does not occur to most of them. And I do not blame them in particular. Their educational institutions have failed them for many reasons both accidental and nefarious.

The ether body is a subtle energetic current or field that is essentially the same size and shape as your physical body. It is responsible for regulating your autonomic biological functions and acting as the liminal permeable membrane between the physical world and the spiritual world. Its most obvious manifestation appears as your chakra system. When you eat food, the thing that knows how to digest it, turn it into useful nutrients, and put those nutrients and energies into the right places is your ether body. It governs your metabolism and does so without you needing to be aware of it. (Imagine if you had to know how to digest food. The level of intelligence necessary to transmute food into energy and physical body mass is beyond anything a human mind or a supercomputer can accomplish. This process is governed by much higher spiritual intelligences.) The reason your heart beats and your lungs breathe without you having to think about it and do it manually is because your etheric body automatically takes care of it thanks to the impulses coming from the spiritual world which govern and sustain your life.

An idea or impulse originates in the spiritual world, it passes into the etheric world, and the ether translates and transmutes it into matter and energy and manifests it out into the material world. The same occurs in reverse. When an alchemist states "As Above, So Below," the comma between these two phrases is the ether.

When a person loses a limb, they often feel that limb as though it were still attached. What they are feeling is their etheric body. Although the material limb is gone, the ether body is much more resilient and retains its shape and place. The etheric body and the physical body are so closely related and similar in so many ways that it can be difficult to distinguish between the two, especially considering that sensations which arise in the nervous system and get translated into percepts for your consciousness to experience are translated not only by the brain, but also by the etheric body. Remember, your consciousness exists in the spiritual world and so in order for a physical sensation to reach your consciousness as a perception, it must pass through the middle world of the ether.

How many bio-medical technologists do you think are considering the ether body when they design prostheses or brain-computer interfaces? I would imagine a number near zero. I have never read an article in a science or medical journal that even approaches this subject. (I could imagine there is a number of very high-end secretive corporations and military projects that do indeed take these things into account, but I doubt we will ever see such things come to the light of day. We will be stuck dealing with whatever the corporate hipsters in Silicon Valley, Seattle and Chicago come up with. Dear Lord, I hope those avocado-toast-eating, modular-synth-playing yuppies learn about this stuff soon.)

Developing technologies which alter the human form without understanding the complete human being is an egregious error. It hearkens back to Gurdjieff's warning about altering a part of yourself before gaining enough self-aware observations: you will put your entire being and even your external world out of balance and it will re-balance itself in harmful and unpredictable ways. You know when you have a bad habit that you become aware of then force yourself to change it, but then something else goes wrong in your life? You develop another bad habit or self-destructive impulse or disorder. That is because you did not observe yourself enough to know where your bad habits originate within you and you changed the symptom without curing the cause. Your being is in total balance and whenever you change something, it will achieve a new equilibrium. If you change it prematurely or incorrectly, the new equilibrium will be just as bad or perhaps even worse than the previous equilibrium. These catastrophes of re-balancing occur a thousandfold when altering our physical bodies in irreversible and permanent ways.

The enormous rates of mental health collapse and suicide of post-operation transgender individuals should alert anyone to the inherent dangers of this type of activity. Please think very carefully about *positive selection* medical procedures before getting them. And make sure you are not mistaking positive selection for *negative selection*. (In the following section a few paragraphs below, I explain positive and negative selection.) This is another enormous issue in today's cultural and identity politics. Many people believe that they are choosing a negative selection with such procedures, thinking that they will be brought to normal human functioning by undergoing such a procedure, when in fact it is an unnecessary positive selection that will alter a normal person resulting in a non-normal outcome. If your physical health is not at risk, a great deal of spiritual and mental guidance, healing and re-balancing should be sought before any permanent medical procedures are decided upon.

(If you suffer from gender dysphoria or body dismorphia, perhaps your Divine Masculine and Divine Feminine spirit is out of balance. Attempt to re-calibrate your inner life through psychological therapy and spiritual disciplines before permanently altering your physical self. You are a beautiful individual just the way you are and you must discover why you are beautiful and lean into it. Embrace it. Do not run from it. If you are a feminine man, so be it. If you are a masculine woman, who cares? You are wonderful. If it truly bothers you, then see about altering your spiritual perspective. You will find infinite strength and happiness when you develop inner balance. I urge you to very carefully consider your choices and courses of action. Seek the opinions, perspectives and counsel from as many professionals and trusted individuals as possible before making irreversible changes to yourself.)

I highly doubt that any bio-medical researchers or technologists understand enough about the etheric body, astral body, mind and spirit to be able to correctly apply genetic, hormonal, mechanical or pharmaceutical alterations to the human body. I imagine we will see a plethora of new mental, physical and spiritual disorders arising from the application of transhumanist technologies. We already see how computers have diminished the attention spans and literacy of many people. Their neural pathways have been shortened, their electrical activity is less, their hormonal excretions are similar to those of drug abusers, and neuronal discharges sometimes fall short of their intended destinations within the brain causing some brain functions to cease working entirely. This is caused just by surfing the internet. Now these people cannot deeply study or engage with anything. They only experience the surface level of all of their perceptions and interests. Depth of experience, thought, feeling, awareness and perception simply does not exist in many millions of people today. Without depth of experience, without sticking to a single topic and digging deeply into it, there is no true knowledge, wisdom or understanding of anything at all. Life itself becomes superficial and banal. People become nothing more than semi-aware animals. Imagine what else is in store for our glorious future once these microchips and processors are no longer just sitting on our desktops or in the palms of our hands but are embedded in our brains and spinal cords.

(An interesting thing to note at this point – take it or leave it – is that the Tradition teaches that humans did not evolve from animals, but that many animals were actually once humans who devolved and fell down the Tree of Life due to poor choices. Next time you see a monkey, just imagine: that could be you in a few thousand years.)

***

The decade of the 1990's was known as *The Age of the Brain* for good reason. Using modern scanning, imaging and detection technologies, researchers were able to peer into the brain of a living person and observe some of its functions in real time on the electrical, thermal, hormonal, mineral, chemical, and electromagnetic levels. Innovators were rapidly able to use this data to wire up the brains of quadriplegics to computers and machines and allow them to actually operate these devices, move the mouse, type words, move a robotic hand and so on, with only their brains and some electrodes. I share in their excitement with these innovations. I do not blame them when they are filled with hope, imagination and wonder at such an incredible thing. It is truly fascinating and may hold the keys to some potentially wonderful therapeutic modalities that could increase general quality of life for those who need them. I would not argue out-of-hand against the obvious benefits for an individual of what is known as *negative selection* of biomedical technologies. (However, there may be a spiritual cost to negative selection, the discussion of which may offend many modernists. We will get to that shortly.)

Negative selection is the use of advancements in medicine to help people who are "below normal" human functioning and bring them to a state of "normal" human functioning. Of course we can argue about what is "normal" and what is not, however; there is a statistical baseline of human functioning that bio-ethicists use as their definition of "normal" – someone with ten working fingers, a working heart and set of lungs that allows them to perform vigorous activity with relative comfort, and so on. The laundry list of "normal" functioning according to academia is obvious with only a few minutes of reflection. Essentially, people who are handicapped may be brought to "normal" functioning through the negative selection (i.e: normal application) of therapeutic and prosthetic modalities and technologies.

There is also the possibility for *positive selection*. This is when a person elects to utilize advancements in medicine to propel themselves from "normal" functioning to "super-normal" functioning. We have seen a version of this with amputee track stars who have replaced their lower legs with these curved pieces of flexible metal. While they may be missing their biological legs, they are in fact able to run faster and farther with less tax on their stamina due to the fact that their bodies do not need to send water, nutrients, blood, oxygen, etc. to their lower legs, their bodies are generally lighter in weight, and their footsteps are of much lower impact due to the clever design of these prostheses.

But positive selection does not end there. Transhumanists consider positive selection to be the future of humanity. They theorize about mechanical shoulder blade wings that will enable personal flight, of replaceable eyeballs that will allow for X-ray vision, augmented reality displays, and so on, of mechanical hands replete with multi-tools and versatile ball joints, of brain implants that offload calculation tasks from the gray matter to the computer processor, of genetic modifications that can alter one's gender or make one taller, stronger, smarter, more talented, etc. Transhuman theorists have vivid imaginations when it comes to all of the things they wish to see humanity do with advances in bio-medical technology. They see positive selection as the road map toward salvation – not only the cure to all woes and ails, but the enabling of the indulgence of all hedonistic desires and the key to taking evolution into our own hands and shaping our future in any way we wish, and doing it quickly.

This impulse can find its origins in the ideas of the ancient (particularly the Renaissance Era) alchemists who wished to use their art to speed up the processes of nature. It is the Hegelian belief that Art is higher than Nature as humanity can use science to more perfectly organize and exploit the processes of nature with greater efficiency, utility and direction. On the face of it, I agree with Hegel. A gardener can grow a magnificent squash by guiding it with the proper controls. It is easy to learn and know what is good for a squash. But is it so easy to learn and know what is good for a human being?

There are countervailing perspectives against the use of many of these bio-medical innovations. Imagine you are a couple and you wish to get pregnant. In the near future, you may be faced with a choice: create a child with love and sexual intercourse or create a child with genetic manipulation and other fertilization methods. The first method comes with the possibility of congenital diseases, birth defects, genetic deficiencies, and other issues that may cause a non-normal person to be born. The other option of gene therapy will insure that the child is healthy, intelligent, has some talent in the arts or some other field, is good-looking, tall, strong, you name it. At first consideration, you may think that of course you would opt for the gene therapy. Most modern people probably would. It is an obvious choice, right? You want the best possible life for your child. But would it really be the best possible life? Are you wise enough to know what the best possible life is for any given individual?

This brings us to the contemplation of unconditional and conditional love. We all know someone with whom we went to school who had parents that only gave them conditional love. The child was only loved and cherished when he performed well in school or in sports or in extracurricular activities or in the work force. If he performed in a lesser capacity than what his parents expected or paid for, the child would be shunned, punished, and left out in the loveless cold. These children generally grow up to be fairly rotten or damaged adults. Any number of psychological and sociological studies of the last one hundred years can demonstrate this.

Now imagine if those same parents designed that child on a genetic level. They paid for him to be the world's best football player, or the greatest mathematician, or the most innovative inventor, or the handsomest model, or the most brilliant scientist, or the most talented musician, or the smartest student in school. His genes are top notch! Now let us imagine he grows up and shows no interest in schoolwork or excelling in his classes. Maybe he decides he would rather live in a Russian monastery and pray to God all day. Or perhaps he does not actually enjoy music and would rather be an auto mechanic. Let us imagine that he decides he does not want to pursue a degree in engineering but would rather open a pottery shop. Maybe he does not want to be a doctor or lawyer and instead would rather pursue life as a woodsman in the wilds of Canada.

It is my bet that these same parents would find less capacity to love their child. They may be wracked with disappointment, resentment and anger. Conditional love may very well increase in a society like this and unconditional love may atrophy and die off. Parents might be filled with all sorts of unrealistic and unfair expectations for their genetically modified offspring.

A person who is conceived naturally through the loving embraces of two parents and is born with disabilities of some kind may require support for his entire life. But have you ever met the parents of such children? The love that flows from them is unfathomable. It is one of the most beautiful things I have ever seen in my life, and just as I am typing this, I am welling up with tears merely thinking about it. They did not genetically design this child. They did not pay for special fertilization technologies to either negatively or positively select traits that would increase the likelihood of "normal" or "super-normal" functioning. They simply fell in love and decided to let God and nature have their say. Whatever type of person they produced would be loved no matter what.

I imagine in a world where genetic modification is common, these parents would be accused of not loving their child, of not wanting the best for them, of not giving their child every chance at a good life. These parents would likely be scolded, ridiculed, mocked, and even banned from certain social functions and societal institutions. Just think about what parents go through today who choose not to vaccinate their children. The exclusion, venom and hatred against them is disgusting and utterly unwarranted to say the least. Parents such as these may face all kinds of social problems for simply doing things the old-fashioned way and having faith that it will work out the way it is meant to. "How dare they put their lives and the lives of their children into the hands of God and not the hands of scientists! Heathens! Filthy mongrels!"

I have even seen parents of handicapped children transform from selfish, petty, horrid people to saints who are capable of bottomless compassion and unconditional love simply because they learned to care for and love their child who was born with non-normal capabilities. It was difficult at first, but they experienced complete inner transformation during these hardships and trials. If they opted in for gene therapy and produced a perfect child, those parents would still be selfish, petty, horrid people. The world would have fewer saints in it. And their child, as perfect as they are, would have experienced a loveless childhood and may develop into a terrible, broken person despite their perfect genes. The handicapped child, although experiencing suffering and limitations in body and mind, experienced a life absolutely filled throughout with unconditional love.

Which is the better life? Which is the worse life? Are you wise enough to determine?

Who is to say what is right and wrong when dealing with the unborn? Who is to say what "quality of life" really means? How can one measure such quality? Is it a biological metric? An economic metric? A social one? A mental one? A spiritual one? Is anyone wise enough to know whether or not to apply these technologies and what consequences may arise? It is my opinion that none of us is wise enough to know the correct choice in any given situation. It must be a carefully considered decision on the part of parents or the individuals who are thinking about applying or not applying such therapeutics and modalities. None of us has a right to either coerce or hinder anyone in this regard.

And anyone considering such things must think beyond just themselves and their selfish impulses. How will gene therapy for their child and transhumanist applications in general affect the rest of civilization, culture, and the future of humanity? Should we take a hands-on approach to our own evolution or a hands-off approach? Should we strike a balance between the two? It all boils down to what type of civilization and culture you want to live in.

***

My fear is the potential stratification of society that may occur if these technologies become widespread. We saw from 2020 onward that there is a desire within the hearts of many people in the general public to stratify society and divide up its accesses and privileges according to whether someone is vaccinated or unvaccinated – according to whether someone believes in modern corporate medicine or is an unenlightened pagan scoundrel. Many governments and people around the world wish to turn unvaccinated people into an underclass, revoking their privileges, depriving them of their rights and considering them to be filthy, inferior, burdensome and dangerous even though in reality they are perfectly healthy and acceptable the way they are. This mentality is the hallmark of every totalitarian tyranny.

Those who have refused the Great and Holy Communion of Vaccination administered by the High Priests of Science in the hallowed church of the medical office are seen as nothing more than pagan heathens and unrepentant sinners in the eyes of the enlightened believers in the truth of government pronouncements, the mass media gospel and the heavenly salvation of modern medicine.

These people will examine the history of the Inquisition, Manifest Destiny, communist revolutions, and the Nazi upheaval and scoff at how stupid and gullible those people were, "How could those people be so selfish and oppressive? How could those normal citizens just go along with that obvious propaganda? I would never be like that!" And then they proceed to call the police on you when they see you are not wearing a face mask, or they kick you out of family dinner night because you did not receive a vaccination. Then they gossip behind your back about how stupid and dangerous your views are. The lack of self-awareness is nightmarish. If they lived in 20th century China, they might have been flag-waving commies publicly shaming people, placing them in stocks and bonds and throwing rotten fruit at them for reading Lao Tzu.

Now imagine a society where there are people who embrace and utilize genetic and technological biological augmentations and there is also a large portion of people who prefer natural human life without any technical tampering. The people who embrace augmentations may have vast physical, mental, political and economic advantages over those who do not. They may even consider themselves to be not only superior to natural humans, but to be an entirely new race of higher beings. The potential for hubris and abuse is astronomical.

Despite these advantages, however; it is very likely that they will have enormous spiritual disadvantages. They have opted in for the easy path of worldly life and will not suffer as often or as readily as a natural-born human. Their inner fortitude and spiritual quality may be greatly diminished due to these material advantages and conveniences. They may not learn forbearance, self-control, forgiveness, unconditional love, psychological adaptation, emotional endurance or the other spiritual faculties that are developed through suffering. We have all seen how pampered, spoiled people fall apart and lose all self-control at the first sign of difficulty and inconvenience. Now imagine if that pampered person had the strength of a bull, the intelligence of a master strategist and the insight of an expert psychologist and then proceeded to become emotionally unhinged while entitled with a superiority complex. The consequences could be devastating for a given culture or community.

Thankfully Gene Roddenberry gave us an entertaining warning about this exact scenario in his *Star Trek: The Wrath of Khan*.

People who prefer the natural life may very well be treated like little more than animals in such a society. My hope is that people are smarter, wiser, and more compassionate than to allow such a society to form. I see indications that they are. I see hope with the number of people who are beginning to see through the biomedical tyranny that has attempted to reshape our culture and society. The corporate medical industry and their financier backers and government lapdogs are largely failing in enforcing their agenda on the masses. The masses seem to possess a very strong and vibrant folk wisdom that irrupts to the surface in times like this, even if they were initially fooled. (Sometimes you need to be deceived once or twice in order to understand the mechanisms of deception and how to protect yourself from them.) Millions are currently coming to their senses about the events of the early 2020's and are turning toward better health modalities despite what governments, corporations, think tanks, and social engineers are attempting to shove down our throats, into our minds, and literally into our bodies. I believe that the natural ethical center that millions of people have found and developed within themselves regarding personal medical decisions will carry over into the future and defend against much of what transhumanists and bio-medical extremists wish to force onto the world.

But not everyone has awoken to the truth of the matter. Society will very likely still split in two: a society of materialistic transhumanists and a society of people who prefer spirit and nature. This may be an inevitable division. "Think ye I came to bring peace? Nay, I came with a sword" (Matthew 10:34.) There are some who really just want to dive head first into the Eighth Sphere. I am not sure if we can help them, or if we even should. The sword of division will likely cut many of us apart from each other. This is one stark reality of spiritual awakening that I have noticed. People leave your life and you leave their lives in droves.

Discuss these topics with your friends and family, make well-considered choices in your own life after seeking opinions from a large number of trusted people and always listen to your heart. Do not put yourself in harm's way trying to rescue people from their own bad decisions. Live and let live except in the most dire of circumstances which require intervention fueled by love, understanding and defense of self and others. Otherwise, let these people do whatever it is that they are going to do. We must not act like inquisitors or enforcers of our own opinions except in those instances where we are asked to and there is a clear desire and request for us to do so.

Personal medical, technological and cultural choices are very delicate subjects and in certain instances, the mishandling of such topics can result in unnecessary conflict and hardship. It is best to remain silent except when absolute necessity arises. Develop your intuition, awareness and discernment so that you may correctly recognize when absolute necessity in fact does arise. And quietly allow those who are going to fall out of your life to fall out of your life.

***

Should society stratify or split in two, given enough time after some generations, a clearly superior civilization and culture will be recognized as such. There is nothing we need to do to make this happen. We need not persuade or coerce anyone into seeing what is right in front of them. It is not up to us to declare which of these two societies is better. We will all judge these trees by the fruits which they may bear. Such things have occurred many times in many great civilizations and we have never had to force the process. Evil sows the seeds of its own destruction. The Good must simply protect itself from Evil's influences and wait for it to destroy itself. The Eighth Sphere will likely be created in this way; it seems to be taking shape right now with these characteristics, and it will simply drop off and away from our world eventually.

Precession of the Equinox

To better understand and gain a solid frame of reference for the shifting and changing of mass opinions, cultural movements, and developments in the human sphere, we need to look at the classical cosmologies and how they change throughout history according to astrological tradition and astronomical time.

During the spring equinox, the Sun rises on the horizon in front of a particular constellation of the Zodiac. And the world is always shifting position in the cosmos so the Sun rises in front of a new constellation about every two thousand years – give or take one or two centuries depending on the size of the constellation. For roughly the last two thousand years, it has risen in the sign of Pisces. A couple of centuries ago, the constellation of Aquarius began slowly moving its way behind the Sun at the spring equinox. We are in the transition period between the Age of Pisces and the Age of Aquarius. It usually takes one to four centuries to be completely out of one Age and firmly in the next.

Each Age is characterized by various traits. Impulses from the spiritual world change from Age to Age. For example, the Age of fast-talking social-butterfly Gemini was characterized by communication and the development of written languages and standardized pictographic representations of concepts. The Age of slow-moving dependable Taurus was characterized by the development of sedentary lifestyles, local economies and animal husbandry. The Age of hot-headed boisterous Aries was characterized by the development of imperial bureaucracy and war. The Age of dreamy and intuitive Pisces was and still is to an extent characterized by religious devotion, faith, emotionality, imagination and belief. The Age of quirky out-of-the-box but very logical Aquarius will be characterized by technology, humanism, individual freedom, ceremonialism and innovations in every sphere of human life. A study of astrology, history, archaeology, epic poetry, religious traditions from all time periods, psychology and anthropology will reveal that the various astronomical Ages really do hold true to the characteristics ascribed to them by the occult lore of astrology. When I was younger, I was reticent to believe it, but as I continued to study all of these fields, it turned out to be a highly accurate way to view general cultural changes over long periods. So it stands to reason that one may be able to predict with some accuracy the future Ages of Aquarius and Capricorn.

Another interesting characteristic of the Ages is that the founding of cities, civilizations, political regimes and religious movements are inaugurated by a ritual sacrifice of a representation of the previous Age while the inaugural prophets and leaders are represented by the symbol of the new age. For example, during the Age of Taurus, the myths about the founding of cities consisted of a pair of twins (Gemini) slaying each other or competing with each other in some way on the site of the original structure of a new city. A famous example is the legend of Remus and Romulus and the founding of Rome. The religious figures and royal rulers of this era were commonly crowned with bull horns or pictographically symbolized by them. During the Age of Aries, religions such as Mithraism, Zoroastrianism and Judaism were founded on the mythology of slaying a bull (Taurus) or destroying an effigy of one. The political and religious leaders were commonly crowned or depicted with ram horns or wore sheep skins and fleeces. In the Age of Pisces, we have the ritual sacrifice of the Lamb (Aries) of God, Jesus Christ and the lamb sacrifices common up to this day in many rites of passage. Jesus and his Apostles were known as fishers of men, Jesus is commonly depicted in ancient statues with fish for feet, he fed masses of people with fish and bread, there is of course his famous legend of calming the seas and walking on water, and the Greek acronym of his name and title is the word for fish: ἸΧΘΥΣ (ichthys) or Ἰησοῦς Χριστός Θεοῦ Υἱός Σωτήρ" (Iēsoûs Khrīstós, Theoû Huiós, Sōtḗr = Jesus Christ, The Son of God,

Savior.) Leaders in the Age of Pisces – the decent ones – took on an attitude of service and self-sacrifice which is of course a deeply Christian ethic and even a fishy one! Salmon move up river to spawn and sacrifice themselves to their unborn children and to the forest and river causing a renewal in the health of the environment. Today, during the inauguration of the Age of Aquarius, industrial civilization is responsible for environmental catastrophes like oil spills, deep sea soundings, river depletion and electromagnetic pollution causing the mass deaths of fish (Pisces) by the billions. This can be seen as a sacrifice on the altar of technological (Aquarian) civilization. New but commonly held ideologies and beliefs are very human-centric and political systems are largely based on demos (the people) and individualism – Aquarius is depicted as a human. Our political leaders are no longer crowned and are considered just one of us. Lord only knows how the Age of Capricorn will be inaugurated considering that the sign of Aquarius is represented by a human being and the sign of Capricorn is commonly used to represent the devil in occult symbolism.

Each Zodiac sign has its dark side. During the Age of Gemini, it was discovered that entire populations could be swayed and deceived with the new technology of the written word and the glyph. Beliefs and fears could be spread like wildfire and whoever commanded the use of the written word was seen as a magician casting spells and controlling reality.

During the Age of Taurus, people learned how to manufacture false scarcity of resources in order to monopolize various industries and economies to gain power over others by controlling the flow of food and goods, corralling people into major urban areas and creating enormous slavish work forces.

During the Age of Aries, warfare was considered an end in and of itself and required no justification aside from bringing glory to one's culture. Loss of life and military catastrophe could occur at any moment anywhere.

During the Age of Pisces, faith was never far from fanaticism. Entire peoples and ways of life were destroyed simply for not conforming to the prevailing ideology of a given region. Ideologies and beliefs arise and cease like trends. The minds of people in this Age were and are very mutable and unstable, easily impressed, prone to fantasy and quickly altered by novel and provocative ideas. When emotions are manipulated, people can be brought to new ideas and belief systems like fish to a lure.

Aquarius is negatively characterized by libertine individualism, selfishness, atheism, disloyalty, infidelity, and innovation for the sake of innovation. Excesses in the pursuit of one's own goals and desires can be expected as the drive toward personal freedom may take precedent over all other social contracts and duties. We see this with the deplorable condition of modern dating and relationships, especially in the West. Sexual deviancy of all kinds can be expected. The desire to innovate can easily lead to the perversion of nature and self. Innovation for the sake of innovation may have no direction, purpose or benefit and can result in the creation of chimeras, golems, useless distractions, aberrations and catastrophic mistakes. The recognition of the power and glory of humanity and our special destiny may result in hubris and self-deification. We may begin to worship ourselves and lose sight of the deeper origins of reality. We see in some corners of the New Age movement that certain people have demoted Tao/God to "The Universe," an inert mass of atoms that possesses only the consciousness which it reflects from ourselves – this seems a bit moribund and self-idealizing to me. We also see it in some places in the world of science and transhumanism where innovators seek to take ultimate power into their own hands and gain absolute control over nature and body to reshape reality into whatever they desire without paying heed to the consequences.

It is no wonder why the Eighth Sphere is becoming so obvious and concerning to occult researchers and spiritual practitioners at this time. During the transition from one Age to another, the dark aspects of those two transitional Ages present themselves so that we may notice and face them, subdue them, and give room for the bright and beneficial aspects of the New Age to manifest in our world. So take heart. This awful period of time has a limit and the benefits of Aquarius will shine through in due course and we will make good use of them as we have in every preceding Age.

The transition between Pisces and Aquarius is particularly strange. When fanaticism meets materialism, when belief meets democratic ideology, when blind faith meets innovation, things can become extremely dangerous and hectic in the mental, spiritual, emotional and physical realms. Political ideologies can come and go as quickly as fashion trends, leaving confusion and devastation in their wake. Technological innovations that we blindly believe will bring us great benefit may turn out to be extraordinarily detrimental and catastrophic to our well-being. The desire to experience the utmost in personal freedom may result in the dissolution of familial and social bonds and the committing of horrible crimes of passion and sadomasochism. The Luciferic spiritual aspects of the Piscean Age are colliding and combining with the Ahrimanic aspects of the Aquarian Age. This is a potent recipe for the acceleration of the creation of the Eighth Sphere. People today are at high risk of being seduced and falling into many different types of delusions and lifestyle aberrations.

It is my hope and expectation that the beneficent aspects of the Aquarian Age will mitigate many of these terrors and detriments in the long term. The ceremonialism of Aquarius will bring orderly standardization to the many newly created ideas, religions, cults, and spiritual movements that so chaotically spawn from the imaginations of people and run rampant today. The Aquarian impulse toward exact science will guide spirituality in general and put emphasis on the spiritual disciplines which have real, repeatable, effective, teachable results. The Tradition may be rediscovered and re-established publicly in this Age, but in a new and innovative way. Those who are familiar with the so-called Occult Revival that began in the 17th century and is picking up steam today will be witness to the chaotic birth pangs of this Traditional re-discovery.

The Aquarian impulse of humanism and individualism will forge the foundation for new social contracts and family structures that are more supportive and nourishing for an individual's creative will and personal expression. A lenience in parental strictures and expectations may result in greater respect for parents from the children and less resentment toward each other, and a reverence for individualism may in fact not atomize a family unit, but glue it together on a new foundation of unconditional love and acceptance as families learn to cherish and celebrate their differences. These differences and quirks may in fact keep families together instead of driving them apart – which unfortunately occurs quite often today due to our unhinged extreme version of individualism divorced from communal bonds. This same reverence and cherishing of differences may also occur on a global scale and we will see the end of globalism and homogenization. The respect for different civilizations with different cultures, different views, different customs, different economies, different beliefs, different goals, different historical missions and so on living side-by-side and tolerating each other may become part of common sense ideology. The West may put aside its incessant and delusional desire to force everyone in the world into becoming Liberal – to force the entire world into becoming The West. We may also see a greater valuation of human life in general. Perhaps the status of people will be raised above the status of the economy and basic needs will be met for all resulting in the eradication of poverty in general. One can dream. (Jacques Fresco was a big influence on me during my formative youth. I see no real reasons why his vision cannot become a reality other than cynicism and greed. If you would like to examine the quintessential inaugural personality of the Age of Aquarius where the faithful compassion of Pisces meets the innovative optimism of Aquarius, you will find an excellent example in the life and work of this man.)

The Aquarian Age brings with it great hope and promise. We must not lose ourselves in the pessimism of the times. We must expand our view to include more than the short timescales of a few years or a single lifetime that we are accustomed to these days. We must view the longer timescales that are behind us and before us and put every movement of history into its appropriate context and witness how seasons of light and darkness ebb and flow. Whenever there is war, peace follows. Whenever there is scarcity, abundance follows. Whenever there is pain, healing follows. Whenever there is dispersal, union follows. Whenever there is winter, spring follows. Whenever there is death, rebirth follows.

Balancing the Extremes

There is a war being waged between the right and left hemispheres of our brains. It manifests in all aspects of human existence: in the world, our society, our laws, our relationships, our actions, our thoughts, our feelings, our beliefs, and our perceptions. This conflict within the seat of our intellectual consciousness has raged longer than we can remember. In our current Age of transition, an opportunity stands before us; a resolution is in sight. This hemispheric war can end in one of a few ways.

The right brain can win and we can do away with technology and metropoli and return to our atavistic lifestyle of hunting and gathering, ruling ourselves with sheer force of will and the excessive mysticism of shamanic pantheism.

The left brain can win and we can replace the workings of nature with machinery, no longer depending on trees to produce our air but fabricating some apparatus that will sink carbon and produce oxygen. Human thought will be seen as fallible and dangerous and will be rendered illegal as we relegate the functions of our hearts and minds to the dictatorial judgments of some artificially intelligent algorithmic machine god; our afterlife being the uploading of our minds to computer processors and hard drives programmed with self-replicating virtual realities.

One path is the indulgence of unhinged mysticism and animalistic urges. The other path is the indulgence of self-image, personal preference and materialism. To a balanced person, both of these paths seem to be the complete derailment of the natural course of spiritual and physical development for humanity and our civilization. These two opposite worldviews and hopes for the future are brought about by delusional Utopian thinking born of absolutism characterized by the unbalanced and excessive dominance of one brain hemisphere over the other. This is why most people do not desire or even think about either of these solutions.

Some may believe that if they lived in an archaic society, they would be perfect little angels roaming naked through the Garden of Eden, eating the ripe fruits plucked straight from the trees, never hurting a fly and waving at all the passersby. (What do a California surfer dude and Adam Weishaupt have in common?) However, there may always be those people who could easily resort to barbarism, cannibalism, sorcery, over-hunting, over-exploiting resources, and hoarding – all of the happy-go-lucky hippies will be carted off to the slave pits, beginning again the terrible cycles of history that we wish to transcend once you realize that self-defense, suppression of evil, and war are necessary parts of life. (People like to give Gandhi and Besant all the credit for liberating India through the practice of satyagraha and non-violent peace protests forgetting that the only reason Gandhi was successful in the south was because there was a full-scale war of rebellion being fought against the English in the north, not to mention, you know, World War Two was going on. This is actually a perfect example of the left brain working with the right brain to accomplish a goal successfully. War and Peace worked in tandem to produce the desired result for a nation.)

On the other side of the spectrum, some may believe that if they lived in a transhuman society, their technology would be the tide that lifts all boats, our lifespans would be increased, diseases cured and the "tyranny of biology" overcome. We could reshape our bodies and lives to suit whatever inane preferences we could dream up. However, it is likely that some augmented tyrant will acquire a superiority complex and decide that those humans who have opted out of augmentation technologies are inferior and ought to be exterminated for the sake of progress. Or perhaps a natural human group will consider augmented people to be abominations and seek to undermine or exterminate them. This sword cuts both ways. Also, the advent of a super-intelligent machine may very well cause an existential catastrophe for the human population. One need only watch a handful of American science fiction films to understand what I mean.

The archaic view is caused by the unbalanced Luciferic impulse of excessive spiritism, excessive fear of God, and unbridled imagination. The transhumanist view is caused by the unbalanced Ahrimanic impulse of excessive materialism, atheism, and unbridled Cartesian compartmentalization – an inability to see the bigger picture.

As I mentioned earlier, when Lucifer operates in his own realm of Spirit, this is fine and natural, but when he encroaches in on material processes, trouble arises and society devolves into theocratic superstition and rebellion.

When Ahriman operates in his own realm of Matter, this is fine and natural, but when he encroaches in on spiritual processes, trouble arises and society devolves into technocracy, materialism and communism (a.k.a. capitalism with fewer consumer choices.)

A Luciferic society is ruled by gods and spirits and leaves no room for human freedom. An Ahrimanic society is ruled by machines and mechanistic processes and also leaves no room for human freedom. An even worse society arises when Lucifer and Ahriman allow each other's excessive influences into their respective realms and begin playing together without parental guidance. An example of an ultimate outcome of the uninterrupted blending of these two impulses, as philosophically wild as it may seem, could be the creation of a demon-possessed supercomputer tentatively dubbed a "machine god" that would dominate every aspect of our lives unto the enforcement of our worshiping of it.

A worse fate can scarcely be imagined. It is even possible that such a fate has befallen races within this universe already. The theory of some alleged government whistle blowers including Lieutenant Colonel Philip Corso and other researchers about the so-called Little Gray aliens (if indeed they are in fact aliens) is that they were once many different diverse, sovereign planetary races thriving throughout the cosmos (some even think that they are time travelers from the future who were once humans on earth), but their interactions with alien technology which was mysteriously and quietly seeded to them from a very patient alien supercomputer led them to develop along lines that were not their own natural path of technical advancement, but were along a foreign path that they were tricked into following. This led to these once-sovereign and diverse races developing technologies which perhaps came from purposely crashed flying saucers and integrating these technologies into every facet of their lives and societies, even their own bodies, deceived into thinking that these advancements came from the brilliant minds of their own inventors when in fact they came from some other source entirely. These mechanical and genetic advancements and alterations eventually led to the subversion and destruction of their uniqueness and sovereignty as they slowly morphed themselves into the genetic aberrations which now appear to us as Little Gray aliens. They thought they were evolving, taking their development into their own hands, progressing their cultures, improving their lives and curing their ills with these technologies, but before they realized their mistake, they had already enslaved themselves to some type of alien machine god who now uses them to expand its homogeneous empire of metal and electricity throughout the stars. They eradicated their own freedom and individuality, their own bodily integrity, and became robot-like – implanted with technologies that allow them to be used as the remote-controlled automata of some strange eldritch horror from beyond known space.

When one reads the hundreds of declassified government reports and the unfathomable number of UFO research books that profess the possibility that technologies like fiber-optics, lightweight high strength alloys and materials, the silicon wafer microchip, and so on may have come from crashed flying saucers, alarm bells might start going off in one's mind. Was it Thomas Fuller who stated that "they which play with the devil's rattles will be brought by degrees to wield his sword?[32]" Perhaps we will be brought by degrees to become his puppets as well.

What a time to be alive! As the kids say. What a time, indeed.

***

If this nightmare scenario is potentially unfolding around us and bodes ill for our own future, and if it is indeed caused by unbalanced and unhinged spiritual and material influences, how might we put this all into balance in accord with our proper development and highest good? We can employ, foster and develop what esoteric philosophers and spiritual practitioners call the Christ Impulse, Buddha Nature, Mithraic Heart, Surya Das, Tiphareth or Solar Spirit (not to mention countless other names.) This impulse which we must allow to arise within our thoughts, feeling and will is the key to keeping Lucifer and Ahriman in their places where they can serve human nature and not subvert it.

An example of how this can be applied on a practical level could mean employing a healthy skepticism of new technologies, slowing down their development to the extent that the common person can wrap their head around it and formulate opinions and best-use scenarios for it in their own lives. Extensive testing and ethical debate can occur during this time and we can democratically or executively decide how to apply, change, or dismiss any given development. For example, if someone were developing personal teleporters, a contra-point to the adoption of this technology could be that we may never stroll through the park, see our neighbors, or have a chance encounter, effectively carving the epitaph on Serendipity's gravestone. A balanced opinion could be that of a person who would use a teleporter to travel large distances and avoid the expenditure of energy resources that would otherwise be used by airplanes, trains and boats, but would elect to continue walking to their local grocery store as to enjoy nature, health, and meetings with neighbors.

How much technological advancement do we really need? Is manual labor really so bad? Do we really want or need to replace human government and decision-making with artificial intelligence? Perhaps a little sloppiness of mind and law and a bit of social danger are some of the costs of freedom. Can we maintain full faith in the sustenance and providence of God while still putting forth technical efforts to improve quality of life for ourselves and each other? Of course God provides our food and water, but it would be wild and unproductive if we were not skilled gardeners and irrigators.

It would be nice if we had institutions open to the public where such questions could be asked and debates could occur. Universities, think tanks, and government councils are abysmally lacking in knowledge, wisdom and openness. There is far too much compartmentalization, specialization, lack of interdisciplinarian communication, ignorance, adherence to old scientific theories, elitism and arrogance in these places. The types of personalities who dominate such proceedings and fora are generally materialists and cork-sniffers who prefer looking at their own framed doctorate degree on their wall than talking with a farmer, a plumber, a cashier, a barista, a dancer, a shoemaker, an accountant, a painter, or anyone else who is seen as "uneducated" or uninitiated or in possession of a valueless and "uninformed" opinion. Yet these are the very people, the common folk of the world, who will be affected most by advances in technologies, and we never have a say in any of it. It is always forced upon us by people who consider themselves great innovators or even our saviors.

Publicly open technological and medical development councils should be a fundamental aspect of all governments, from the most local level to the largest regional level. Peasant wisdom is generally the most important and valuable type of wisdom, yet it is generally disregarded and ridiculed in today's society. This attitude must change. Sometimes, the least educated people have the deepest and most practical wisdom. A farmer may not have a doctorate in applied mechanical engineering, but he is the one who knows what kind of tools he wants to use. A musician may not hold a doctorate in neural science, but his brain is more active than any other person's brain. A proprietor of a tea house may not hold a doctorate in sociology, but she knows how to make people laugh and feel at home.

I am not sure of your opinion, but I, for one, have reached my limit with armchair philosophers, university-cloistered "disruptors" and a scientific community which has devolved to its logical conclusion: a self-congratulating circle jerk rewarding themselves for solving problems which they created in the first place. The Wheel of the World turns and now that it is rimmed and studded with technologies that are too difficult for the average person to understand or use in a healthy balanced way, it crushes all those who take even one misstep into its plowing path. The Wheel of Dharma must turn now, too, and put a halt to this technological arms race, to slow down and allow the human soul to catch up and come to terms with the changes of the last five centuries. Judgment must be cast onto the world. The common people, having filled their hearts with the Holy Spirit, must stand tall, put their palm out and say, "No." Refuse to supplicate before this tide of so-called "progress" and do not allow your humility to become humiliation. Everybody tells us that we need to adapt to the changing times. Of course adaptation is good when it is for a good cause and has a healthy outcome, but you should not adapt to evil. Evil must be noticed, recognized, and resisted – not tolerated. Criticize those aspects of society which deserve criticism, applaud those which deserve applause and suppress that which must be suppressed. If your heart is telling you that something is wrong, then it is probably wrong. Adopt and use those things which you know are for your highest good and avoid those which would bring you harm.

Be innocent as doves, and shrewd as snakes.

Putrefaction and Advent: The Rise, Fall and Rebirth of Institutions and Cults

There is great danger in the avoidance and hindrance of the discussions, debates and councils that I believe should be held uninhibited and publicly, as I mentioned in the previous chapter. The danger is a thousandfold when these debates and discussions fail to occur during the collapsing stages of a civilization such as ours.

If you do not believe that our civilization is indeed collapsing, simply look around you. Reflect on the last two hundred years of Western civilization and compare it to the historical records of other collapsed civilizations and recognize the inherent patterns. Thinkers such as Julius Evola and Oswald Spengler[33] have sufficiently explained and proven this fact. But I do not blame you if it is difficult to recognize. When one civilization is collapsing – an event that can take up to five centuries – another civilization can oftentimes be born from within the dying one, and it is possible that no one will notice that their culture and society has died until they have been firmly established in the new one for a few centuries. One day, they will open their eyes and realize that the values and attitudes of their ancestors are no longer held or enacted by the current generation. This is when you will know that the culture you believed you were a part of in fact no longer exists and you are in actuality a member of a new civilization that grew up around you without anyone realizing it. For example, how many people live their lives according to a code of chivalry and knightly conduct? How many people live by the virtues of chastity and fidelity? How many people live by faith and modesty? In the West, this number is a pitiable minority. Western values have essentially died or, at the very least, are on life support in the hearts and minds of people who are derided as "old school" and for having "outdated" or "problematic" beliefs.

A new civilization is being born from the corpse of the West. As the tomb of King Arthur cracks and splits and becomes overgrown with moss and foliage, the outer surroundings are being paved over, the forests and hills are being replaced with industrial metropoli, the people who used to leave flowers and offerings at the sarcophagus are now spraying graffiti on it and using its damp shelter as a drug den, and it is only a matter of time before the tomb itself is condemned as a safety hazard, demolished, and replaced with a new internet server farm that services online bankers. A reincarnation of Galahad who feels the urge in his soul for authenticity and chivalric heroism approaches the corporate server farm and loudly bemoans the end of the Golden Age of the Round Table, weeping on a piss and oil-stained sidewalk, shouting at clouds that he can find no Grail

Knights to accompany him on his quest for enlightenment and spiritual power as onlookers record the troubled man with their cell phones and post mocking commentary about him on social media until the police show up, subdue him, and send him to a psychiatric institution.

So goes the Last Westerner.

Thus ends the West.

And no one notices. No one cares. They still have full refrigerators. The electricity in their homes still works. They are still employed. They are distracted by their internet connections and entertainments. They are going out on dates this weekend. They are graduating from school next month. No one sees what has died. No one sees what has been born. It happened too slowly and surreptitiously. There was no great cataclysm – no moment of great import. One culture simply petered out and morphed into another. One value was forgotten and replaced by a new value. One custom was abandoned and replaced by a new custom. This process went on slowly over many generations, one value at a time, one custom at a time, until there were no more values or customs from the original West left in anyone's heart or mind. There are only the new values and the new customs which belong to a new culture, a new civilization. How did this new culture and civilization come to be? Where does its impulse originate? Why did it happen almost unconsciously on the part of the masses?

***

The decomposition of one form of life is the crucible for another. There is more diversity of life inside the trunk of a dead tree than there was within the living tree. Though the diverse forms that churn within the dead wood seem grotesque to our delicate modern sense of aesthetics, without them, the soil would be deprived of essential nutrients and fertilizer and no new plants would grow. This is the material manifestation of the alchemical process of putrefaction. It is a natural and desirable process that occurs at opportune times in a holistic ecosystem.

However, on rare occasion, an alien germ may penetrate this churning crucible of new life and, while its fructifying ability to multiply and spread may not be diminished, the essential quality of this new life may be corrupted. When the birds, animals, insects, and fungi come to take their share of this rich source of biomass and deposit it throughout the forest as is their wont, they will not be spreading vitality or reinvigoration but a disease that may threaten the entirety of the forest itself.

This process occurs on social and civilizational scales as well. It is less of a metaphor and more of a precise analogy. As human beings endowed with reason, we have the responsibility to notice and examine all crucibles of putrefaction that appear from time to time in our world. When institutions, be they religious, economic, political, social, or what have you, begin to collapse and corrode, we must be vigilant and notice that it is in fact happening, and instead of sticking our heads in the proverbial sand and ignore it or complain about it, we must proactively guide the process and protect the decomposing matter from toxic germs and only allow those germs which we believe will be of benefit to the fertilizer that will be made. We must be mindful and properly cultivate and purify such crucibles so that their products are in line with truth and virtue.

When a civilization is in a state of decay, new ideas, new political organizations, new cults, new economic systems, new sciences and such like begin to manifest generally unseen or unrecognized at first, in the margins and fringes, subterranean, and they are usually despised and ridiculed by the mainstream when they come to the light of day. Most of these new enterprises and phenomena will fizzle out and die like the worthless slough that they are. However, some of these will become the very foundation of the new civilization that will overthrow the old. As conscious individuals, we had best keep abreast of such developments.

The marginalized contents and hardworking microbes in the crucible may be hard at work creating a disease and spreading corruption that is largely unseen and unrecognized, festering under the surface, and when the symptoms become obvious, it may already be too late.

Somewhat less than two thousand years ago, global civilization was largely governed by a form of imperial rationalism and pragmatism with overtones of polytheism. Society was rigid and mysticism was bureaucratized and formalized. In the fringes and margins of this society, a cult was emerging – a cult that glorified martyrdom and poverty, a cult that very publicly raved about the collapse of civilization on an all-consuming scale brought about by supernatural beasts of horrible aspect and tremendous power – a cult that heralded a Utopia that would be built especially for them by their new god which would replace the current degenerate society. A most bizarre and ridiculous belief, to be sure. This cult was suppressed in the extreme, its members being fed to lions for sport, their towns being burned to the ground, and their doctrine and dogma being dissected, ridiculed, and criticized by the greatest scholars and satirists of the time. But these obstinate people failed to recognize the growing popularity of the doctrines and beliefs of this cult, and in their inflexibility and inability to adapt to and recognize this cultural shift, they permitted this cult to infiltrate the very lifeblood of their civilization and all of its institutions. The cult would increase in number and potency quietly like gangrene in an unsuspecting victim. In no more than three centuries, Roman civilization would be usurped and overthrown by the irrational superstitions of the Catholic Church which would come to dominate the world through fear, violence, coercion and treachery for nearly fifteen hundred years.

Never underestimate any fringe group who can evoke a mystical devotion from their adherents, no matter how ridiculous, outlandish or laughable their dogma may seem. One day, it may take a few centuries, but one day they may become the very world order that governs our civilization for the foreseeable future.

What comes to mind now is a phenomenon that has existed perhaps no earlier than the 1950's, though there were murmurs of its advent in the 1870's when its first prophets and doctrines appeared. I am referring to the vexing and embarrassing UFO cults. As laughable and ridiculous as their doctrine and dogma may seem, we would be remiss to ignore this global phenomenon out of hand, for there are within our governments and businesses today influential individuals who are firm, even fanatic, believers in Blavatsky's Theosophy, Bailey's Agni Yoga,

Roerich's Agartha, Ballard's "I Am," Adamski's Space Brothers, Roberts' Seth Material, *The Urantia Book*, Ballou's *Oahspe*, and many other New Age extra-terrestrial-themed pseudo-religions.

There are numberless UFO and New Age cults throughout the world, all with their own leaders, mediums, channelers, and prophets, and while they seem superficially different, and indeed sometimes they even have spiritual and legal battles against each other, they are in fact alarmingly similar in their methods and goals, so much so that I suspect some sort of subtle and adept network of organization.

(I am not saying that all these groups are full of it, but as someone with extensive experience traveling throughout India and the Western world in search of authentic spiritual masters and teachings, and as someone who has done lifelong research into religious, spiritual, philosophical and scientific matters, it has been my experience that the vast majority, perhaps as many as ninety percent of gurus, yogis, channelers, psychics, spiritual leaders, laboratory scientists and science commentators are frauds and liars recognized as such by the application of judging a tree by the fruit it bears. Of the remaining ten percent who have authentic supranormal experiences, most of them are being led down the garden path by tricksters or their own delusions. Authentic spiritual masters who act as leaders of authentic groups are extraordinarily rare. And when one of the good leaders who sits at the head of a group dies, the group immediately degenerates into in-fighting, delusion and falsehood – the authenticity vanishes with them.)

***

I would like to address the UFO phenomenon itself and its uncanny ability to invent new cults which appear spiritually oriented, but are in fact veiled materialism.

The UFO phenomenon is a very real phenomenon – inarguably so. Anyone who denies this has simply not experienced it first hand. It has psychic, spiritual and physical aspects and possesses the capability to distort the perceptions of reality of contactees and witnesses. The scientific community ought to take this more seriously than it does any other phenomenon. There ought to be entire institutions dedicated to this investigation. Instead, scientists dare not touch the subject with a thirty-foot pole and proceed to ridicule and destroy the careers of those who are interested in investigating this subject. This fact is disturbing and dangerous in the highest degree. It is a gross manifestation of arrogance, ignorance and negligence. (Of course, there are studies and institutions which exist in secret, underground, and you can join one if you are deemed worthy. Just be sure to read the fine print.)

Millions of people the world over have had and continue to have highly strange experiences that they cannot explain – experiences of luminous objects from the sky and encounters with bizarre otherworldly intelligences and absurd alien forms of consciousness. They seek answers, reconciliation, understanding, and peace of mind like anyone would. The scientific community arrogantly ridicules and disregards these people and obstinately refuses to help them search for answers. In their dogmatic and fanatical adherence to rationalism and materialism, the scientific community has driven UFO researchers, witnesses and contactees away from science and into the clutches of fantasy, delusion, unhinged mysticism and predatory cults. People will seek answers wherever they can get them, especially if they are traumatized and desperate, rendering themselves vulnerable to deception and danger.

I urge all individuals who are open-minded and healthily skeptical, who have a strong spiritual foundation all the while subjecting their perceptions to the rigors of science, to investigate the UFO phenomenon, paranormal occurrences, and the cults associated with them. The direction in which our civilization develops may very well be in your hands.

We are still early in the 21st century and the clear and present danger of New Age UFO cults should be abundantly obvious. Jim Jones and his Heaven's Gate cult committed mass suicide and homicide in order to catch a ride on an extraterrestrial mothership. The Order of the Solar Temple also committed mass murder and suicide in order to "ascend to the next level." A woman was murdered and her corpse desecrated for the sake of providing an autopsy for an alien zoologist from the planet UMMO by someone who was involved in a cult that used hypnotism and mental suggestion[34]. Countless are such tales from the annals of this transition into the New Age. The same sorts of things occurred when the Age of Aries changed to the Age of Pisces, and before that when Taurus turned to Aries, and before that...

While the cults mentioned above have dissolved and will likely never rise again due to their outward and obvious barbarism, there are nonviolent cults which are far more popular yet retain a similar and perhaps ultimately more dangerous dogma.

Annie Besant's version of Theosophy and Alice Bailey's Agni Yoga can very nearly be described as mainstream religions in the Western world considering how widely and discreetly their dogma has been adopted by almost all New Age groups and even some scientists and politicians. While up to eighty or ninety percent of their doctrines may very well be true, it is the remaining few percent which contains the poison of lies that will reap the damnation of its practitioners.

(As harshly critical as I am of Helena Blavatsky, Theosophy and similar New Age movements, I would like to point out that I believe there has been a net benefit to the world due to the existence and work of these people and their groups, from which I have benefited and for which I am very grateful. But we must not ignore the subtle influences of dark powers that sneak their way into these things. Thankfully, when the devil sows the seeds of tares and weeds, God has a way of transmuting them into flowers for honey bees.)

Theosophy (at least in its second wave) and Agni Yoga teach the so-called "permanence of the atom." This dogma, as revealed to Besant and Bailey by non-corporeal "Ascended Masters" whose identities have never been verified, describes that the soul and the spiritual world are nothing more than very rarefied matter – that the basis of reality is the atom and to enter the spiritual world, one must simply raise the vibration of their body and soul. This is extremely popular terminology in today's spiritual marketplace.

Any spiritual practitioner worthy of the title knows that "raising your vibration" (as vague a concept as that is at first glance) certainly aids in approaching the spiritual world, and is a necessary step, but it does not allow access to it. There is a strict divide, an abyss that must be crossed, an etheric membrane, between the worlds of Matter and Spirit. The spiritual world is entirely immaterial. The only matter contained within the spiritual world is the material world itself – like an ice cube floating in a glass of water. Technically the ice and water are essentially the same element (just as Spirit and Matter are both Tao), however; a solid is not a liquid and a liquid is not a solid. In order for ice to become water, it must entirely lose its solid nature and become utterly liquid. Ice is not permanent. It becomes the liquid. An atom is not permanent. It becomes Spirit.

This insidious little bit of doctrine has the potential to deceive and derail honest spiritual seekers. It can confuse and misdirect a person's entire spiritual journey right at the onset – especially if one is intellectually oriented and seeks spiritual enlightenment through primarily mental means such as in the discipline of jnana yoga. At first glance, especially from the perspective of a Western-educated materialist, it has a sort of mystical logic and is a seductive idea given that when we consider the Superspectrum, things that have a higher vibration are indeed subtler and more energetic. It could logically follow that those higher vibration energies are in fact spirit itself. But to consider the atom to be the foundation of spirit is the same argument that the brain is the foundation of consciousness. This way of thinking will cause spiritual development to come to a screeching halt. It may even change a spiritual seeker into a materialist without their realizing it, which I believe, in my paranoid little mind, was the goal of these so-called "Ascended Masters" all along. I think they were deliberately attempting to subvert and undermine Western civilization by implanting these ideas and lead it into a political disadvantage in the realm of geopolitics by demoralizing and misleading the spiritual practitioners and bright minds of the West. Sergei Prokofieff has written an excellent dissertation on this[35].

Gurdjieff also warned, and I agree because I have seen it, that those who put Theosophy into practice as a spiritual path or as a way of thinking of oneself become deluded and self-important. It has the effect of expanding one's ego and giving it more control over one's life. The person will believe that they are on a special mission, that they have been anointed, that they are part of a more advanced and evolved race of humanity, that they have been especially selected by higher beings, and that this is of utmost importance because they are the only ones who can develop humanity and the earth, no one else is capable – it inculcates a sense of stressful urgency and a superiority complex. This self-image and its attendant mission becomes of paramount importance to the direction of their lives and they will fail to dissolve the aspects of their personality which must be dissolved. They become attached to these aspects because they believe these character traits are necessary for some great human destiny. Their self-awareness practice will be distorted and prevented from achieving success.

Though thankfully this intellectual trap is more of a 19th - 20th century problem. Many New Agers have lately developed a great deal of discernment regarding this in a very short period of time, which is very inspiring and hopeful in my opinion. Because many New Age spiritual practices begin from heart-centered thinking and willing and root chakra healing, there is actually far less likelihood of stumbling into intellectual traps in general. Starting your spiritual journey with the heart and root creates an intuitive insurance program – basically heart-centered, root-supported practices develop your bullshit detector.

This doctrine of the "permanence of the atom" is another stark example of the Luciferic spiritual impulse merging with the Ahrimanic material impulse leading to the derailment of organic development and diverting it into fantasy or delusion. Many New Agers, especially in the 19th and 20th centuries, wanted (and some still want) so desperately to be taken seriously by the scientific establishment and a mainstream audience that they adopt scientific terminologies and apply it to their occult teachings, throwing around words like "quantum" and "atom" and "dark matter" and "plasma torsion" looking for that nod of approval from some stuffed-shirt in an Ivy league gown or hoping to get a grant committee to sign a check. Instead of attempting to gain acceptance in the current paradigm's establishment, our time and energy would be better spent building the new paradigm's establishment.

Another alarming example of Lucifer and Ahriman placing their influence over a prophet of the Space Brothers concerns Claude Vorilhon a.k.a. Raël. He formed a UFO cult in 1973 after he had a chat with a UFO occupant named Yahweh (red flag, anyone?) who told him that the Elohim of Biblical tradition are in fact extraterrestrials from another planet who are just like humans except about twenty five thousand years more technologically advanced, and their genetic scientists are responsible for creating earthly humanity. (I guess we may never outgrow etiological myth-formation.) In this cosmology, the gods and angels have been reduced to flesh-

and-blood people and spiritual experiences are reduced to alien encounters. This cult is also heavily invested in human cloning research and other biomedical corporate ventures.

This brings me to an issue that seems prevalent in many New Age cults. There seems to be a great interest in eugenics and totalitarianism hidden within some of the New Age movement. Many New Agers would vehemently deny any accusations of superiority complexes in one breath, then in the next breath they will tell you about which Starseed they are and why they so graciously and benevolently decided to sacrifice their wonderful life in a Utopian heaven-world to incarnate as a human in this fallen hell-hole of a world in order to bring us enlightenment, peace, and happiness and to show us how to activate our lesser DNA and evolve to the next level of ascension and greatness.

Alright, so you decided to slum it with the heathens in order to carry out your great mission of civilizing the savages and bringing genetic advancement? Queen Victoria called, she wants her missionary pamphlets back.

Need I remind the reader of the Ariosophists within the Vril, Thule and Lizard Societies who utilized a handful of attractive female trance channelers to allegedly convey messages from advanced space-faring humans who filled their minds with delusions of grandeur that they were descendants of these very same advanced extraterrestrials from Aldebaran? Inspired by these messengers from the outer worlds, they then created the Order of the S.S. and puppeteered the Nazi regime. How long will it be before the New Age hippies get impatient with our barbarism and trade in their crystals and scented candles for panzer tanks? The Germans were all peace and love and *blumenkraft* from the 1870's to the 1930's... and then they weren't...

Who knows? Maybe they were right. Maybe they were the good guys in World War Two. Perhaps we should have let them civilize us savages. What do I know? But my point is that paranormal encounters sometimes act as major forces of social engineering which cause massive upheavals in geopolitics, cultural development and historical processes. For better or worse. Remember Constantine and the cross in the sky and the centuries of warfare and repression that followed.

Perhaps you think I am being alarmist, but all it took was about a dozen well-placed members of a secret society to hijack a cultural revival movement and change it into a machine of war. If you have ever wondered why intelligence agencies and secret societies (both private and governmental) infiltrate New Age groups, this is why. Some wish to prevent a new

Hitler, some wish to create one.

* * *

All this talk about Space Brothers, Ancient Aliens, Ascended Masters and Starseeds for the last century has implanted within the minds of the masses that humans are just too stupid, incapable, dissonant, violent, and irredeemable when left to our own devices. We need an intervention!

If you peruse the internet, social media, blogs, discussion fora or news websites, you will find the sentiment everywhere coming out of the mouths of elite think tanks, celebrity personalities, and common folk alike that we need benevolent aliens to invade and take responsibility for us, that we need to give away all of our sovereignty to some foreign beings because they must be smarter and wiser and better than us in every way. We need to take power out of our own hands and put it in the hands of some all-wise space aliens! This is a mental and cultural implantation that was put here by the UFO cults of the 20th century and their intelligence agency handlers (or are they the ones who were handling the intelligence agents? Chickens and eggs.) Where once this was merely the strange messianic ramblings of fringe personalities whose ranting and raving was largely ignored during the Eisenhower administration, now has taken root in the hearts of common people who may never have even heard of any UFO cults. This was the same development of the early Christian movement as it spread, standardized, misrepresented and abused its own ideology and transformed into the Catholic Church and dominated the world shortly thereafter through violence and oppression. That movement began innocently enough until Emperor Constantine and a couple of think-tank meetings set the precedent of wielding the cross like a sword.

The same way that the early Christian movement heralded the end of one civilization and the beginning of a new one (and they were correct because they made it happen like a self-fulfilling prophecy), so too is the UFO cult aspect of the New Age movement. How many military officers, politicians, celebrities, corporate board members, church officials, school teachers, and so on profess a belief in space aliens? How many of them believe that these aliens are likely more advanced and wiser and more benevolent than humans? That they must come from wonderful Utopian worlds and have solved all the problems of governance? A few decades ago, this would have been a tiny number, but these people have infiltrated every facet of our society, every institution of our civilization, and today that number is surprisingly large. These true believers are everywhere now.

Where once they were proverbially fed to lions, now they are writing our laws and teaching our youth.

Where once they were ridiculed and laughed at, now they own the world's most powerful corporations.

Imagine another fifteen hundred years of repression, inquisition and terror as these believers prepare the world for the coming of their messianic Space Brothers. "The ships are on their way! We promise! Any day now! Just do what we tell you, give us all your money and political power and everything will work out just fine! But they'll only save us if you really, really believe!"

Now imagine if there actually was some mass UFO phenomenon that occurred all around the world all at once. Perhaps it will be made to look like the Second Coming of Jesus, or maybe like the arrival of the Space Brothers, or the coming of Kalki Avatar, or perhaps it will look like an enemy flotilla of alien ships invading with weapons in attack position and attempting to conquer us. I would not be surprised if this was the ace up someone's sleeve, just waiting for the world to be primed for a mass illusion. Imagine if the Eighth Sphere has collected enough matter and energy and has built up a store of enough power to produce such an illusion on a physical level, perhaps secretly with the help of military officials, technologists, and other true believers who were promised a reward for their help. This is the sort of deception that researchers like Rudolf Steiner and C.G. Harrison warned could potentially happen in this time period if we were unable to develop enough discernment in time. The Eighth Sphere could potentially impose itself on us as a global government of aliens, ascended masters, angels, and saints – all of whom would be no such things. They would wear these disguises to conquer us without firing a single shot. They might not even exist in the discrete sense; they could be egregores – projections of some unknown will or secret technology.

***

The first stage in conquering an enemy population is to spend years infiltrating, disrupting and demoralizing them – to get them to desire foreign leadership. Getting a population to hate and doubt themselves, to consider themselves weak and powerless through false spiritual teachings, falsified history, economic sabotage, demoralizing propaganda, and psychological trickery has been a tactic of secret societies and conquerors for thousands of years. I see these same tactics being used against us right now. I do not know exactly by whom, but I can see their activity in the same way I cannot perceive the wind directly, but I know its presence and activity by watching it blow the window curtain. They use everything at their disposal, every institution available to them. They use academia, science, government, business, media, religion, and every other place where people go for community, protection, sustenance, culture and knowledge. Do you truly believe that the New Age movement has been spared this sort of infiltration and social engineering? I follow Murphy's Law of Conspiracy: if they *can* do it, they *are* doing it.

The War on Consciousness

Drugs are bad, mmkay? When you are high, you cannot go to work. You cannot sit in a cubicle in front of a computer. You cannot operate industrial machinery. You cannot deal with customers. You are very unproductive. You would rather sit in a sunny flower field and talk to pixies. In short, you cannot make money for the boss!

How can you participate in a technological industrial civilization if you insist on eating shrooms and smoking weed all the time? We cannot have this. We must make these things illegal – unless we figure out how to use these things to control the masses, maybe after we develop our own genetically modified or botanically altered versions of these things that produce the mental effects we desire which will dull the population into complacency and stupidity. Then we will legalize them, but only our versions will be sold for consumption as we quietly destroy the original seed stock.

The Illuminati said this in the 1960's. Probably.

Most people believe that recreational drugs are illegal because they are toxic and unhealthy. But honestly ask yourself, how much does the American government care about your health? I will save you the time: not at all. Most of the hard drugs that are ingested in this country are trafficked to us by the talented entrepreneurs in the Central Intelligence Agency, you know, those guys who work for the government. They enjoy giving us mixed signals about these things. It gives them a good chuckle. The laws against drugs are just a way for them to make money. They make money selling drugs, they make money incarcerating the drug sellers and users, then they make money from the rehabilitation centers that they so philanthropically open for all the poor suffering addicts. They are making money out of both ends. Honestly, you have to admire their tenacity.

There is another reason for the various laws about drugs in the United States, and to understand them, we can take a glance at the "scheduling" of substances categorized by the Drug Enforcement Agency. Basically, according to the DEA, Schedule I drugs are the most dangerous and come with the greatest potential for abuse while Schedule V drugs are the least dangerous and have the least potential for abuse[36]. Now I will ask you, where do you think psilocybin mushrooms and marijuana fall in this scheduling? Schedule V? Maybe IV? They couldn't possibly be III or higher? Could they?

Well, they are in fact Schedule I, along with LSD, MDMA and peyote. On Schedule II, we find cocaine, meth, oxycodone, and fentanyl (you know, the one that immediately kills you when you snort it.) According to the Great Wise Ones in the Federal Government, things that grow in your backyard like weed, shrooms, and cactus hearts are more dangerous than the highly addictive, toxic and fatal synthetic drugs listed above.

Why is it that these virtually non-toxic and non-addictive drugs are considered so dangerous according to the government? How often do police drag out an overdose victim's corpse from a marijuana cafe? When do you see peyote junkies stabbing each other in alleyways for money? How often are shroom whores turning tricks for another cap? The answer is virtually never. But we see these horrors of modern society every day with the poisonous drugs listed in the less severe schedules.

The scheduling is obviously not according to toxicity or biological health dangers. Again, the government cares about your health about as much as a flesh-eating virus does – it is only important to them to the extent that they can feed off of it. (There are actually some fungi and viruses that keep their victims in a weakened and sickly state but just alive enough so that they may feed off of them in perpetuity. I see where the American Federal Government gets its inspiration.)

So if the scheduling is not about physical

effects, then it must be about mental effects. Cocaine addicts can still make great bankers and can have a very productive attitude. Marijuana smokers and shroom eaters, not so much. Oxycodone and Adderall will dull people's pain and give them the numbness and focus necessary for menial tasks so they can get back to work after they receive an injury or experience some mental disorder. Someone who has a self-aware epiphany caused by a weekend in the desert with a stomach full of peyote may quit their corporate job, tell society to kiss his ass and stop paying taxes. Consuming an entheogen can be similar to putting on those glasses from the classic John Carpenter film *They Live*. Of course, those glasses are illegal, too.

Basically what has happened here, is that the government have taken it upon themselves to render different states of consciousness illegal. You are only allowed to experience those states of consciousness which render you easily manageable and productive in a society that has raised the economy to the level of Godhood. (Now the word "government" makes so much more sense! It is a simple Latin phrase. Govern: to control. Ment: mind. It literally means "mind control." Just throwing that out there.)

It is forbidden for you to experience altered states of consciousness. It is forbidden for you to stop participating in the economic system.

It is forbidden for you to explore your own perceptions. The only ways in which you may alter your consciousness are with the synthetic pharmaceuticals that transform you into a good little citizen who gets back to work and copes with their slavish and miserable existence. Any drugs that would allow you to instantly see through the illusion of our horrible, evil and degenerate civilization are considered the most dangerous drugs in existence. And you know what? They probably are the most dangerous... for corporations, governments, and other tyrants of all sorts who rely on your fear, hatred and ignorance to maintain their own power. If everyone checked out and chilled out, they would lose all the control they have over us. Imagine if we all decided not to go to work, that we all just wanted to sit around and hang out, that we don't want to pay or accept money for anything, who cares? There's so much stuff everywhere! Why pay for it? We actually can't even understand what money is, it's just a bunch of green paper, what the hell even is paper? Listen to the swishy sound it makes! Heh! Do I have seventeen fingers? Why do you have an extra eye moving around your forehead? You hungry, man? Let's share some food. Has anyone told you that you're beautiful today? I'm never going back to that cubicle. My boss can go kick rocks! Look at that sunset! Wow! I think God is in all of our hearts, right now! I think I can see

Him!

You can imagine how the power structures of society would evaporate if we all tripped balls together at the same time. This is the real reason why these drugs are illegal and placed on this highest schedule. We would all become unmanageable and unemployable.

As I mentioned in an earlier chapter, I do not condone the use of drugs except under therapeutic and specialized circumstances with the guidance of trustworthy individuals and experienced professionals. I think there are better ways of cultivating love, unity and spirituality within yourself. But I'm not your mom. Do what you want.

***

I simply wish to illustrate the point that your mind is being controlled and corralled by other people and forces. Even when you are not directly being brainwashed, you are being led and sometimes forced to walk down only the most narrow corridors through life and consciousness without you even realizing that it is happening. This means that those other people and forces are absolutely terrified of what you and your mind are capable of. They know that if you unleashed and expanded your consciousness to even a fraction of its full most holy potential, you would put them in their place; they would lose all their power, they may even be horribly punished for all that they have done to us over the centuries.

If you find it difficult to be motivated in your spiritual development because the idea of self-improvement or self-knowledge is just not enough of an inspiration to get you going; be motivated by the need to suppress evil. Develop your spiritual faculties for the goal of becoming a warrior of light and rendering evil powerless in this world. Not all of us are here to be healers and drum circle dancers (unless that's your thing! We need those people, too!) Some of us need to draw swords, either metaphorical or real. But before you can conquer the demons in the outside world, you must explore your consciousness fully and conquer your inner demons. Only then are you worthy of wielding any sort of intellectual or actual weapons.

As long as the exploration of consciousness is stifled by the enemies of humanity, the world will have a minimum of true warriors.

The dark powers of this world corrupt and twist the realms of medicine, technology, religion, science, media, academia and social interaction in order to create the Eighth Sphere, a prison in which they wish to put us all. The suppression of your mind, your consciousness, is absolutely crucial for their agenda to be successful. The news media will attempt to make you angry and afraid, then the government and corporations step in and offer you a ready-made solution to that exact fear and anger – but that solution will eliminate one more of your liberties, it will insult and oppress one more aspect of your dignity. Academia will force you into believing that two and two make five and insure that you will never earn money if you insist that those numbers actually make four. They will threaten you with poverty, loneliness and chastisement in order to keep you participating in their Great Society, to make sure you work as a cog in their machine. Your mind is attacked constantly from all quarters and this assault begins in childhood. This is a dark and vile Age in which we live and it has been this way for so long that we find it difficult to imagine any other type of world, and when we do, we are attacked even more ruthlessly for daring to think that there could possibly be any other worlds better than this one.

All you need to do is notice that this suppression is occurring to you. As soon as you say, "I don't want this," then the keys to your prison cell appear in your hand and you can simply step out of your confinement. (8 of Swords energy, right here.) There will be struggle and difficulty, especially against your own ego wishing to preserve itself in its earlier more ignorant and arrogant state where it felt safe. You may also lose friends and family who are no longer sympathetic with you. Your views will change, you will change, and people will leave your life and may even actively dislike you. So be it. They are no longer your people. This is all part of awakening your consciousness. This is all part of stepping away from and rejecting the Eighth Sphere.

But other things will leave your life as well: your fear of the government, your fear of the news and events of the world, your hatred for other people, your unease about the future, your lack of confidence to speak your mind, your fear of being judged by normies. You will let go of everything that was holding you back, like a plant whose roots have grown too large for its pot and must find new, richer, wider tracts of fertile land in which to grow and live. Your pot may shatter, and you will need to be careful when walking through the broken shards, but then you enter the forest and open fields where you can discover who you really are. And you will grow large and strong enough to the point where you will bear fruit.

The free forests and fields contain their own mysteries, dangers and predators. Awakened individuals tend to find a whole new army of enemies who are out for their blood. But it is my opinion that it is better to be under threat and free than to be secure and imprisoned, because that secure-seeming prison is not as safe as it may appear. It is replete with parasites who will drain you and spiritual blockages that will unravel you over time and is in fact far more dangerous than this proverbial spiritual wilderness. Some parasites make us feel comfortable; they inject us with chemicals that subdue us and tranquilize us so we end up not minding or noticing that they are consuming our life force. Notice that these chemicals are coursing through your veins, find the parasites which do this to you and cut them out of your life.

The best place to start is by limiting your use of and distancing yourself from modern technologies like computers, phones, and televisions. These devices alter your neural chemistry and neuronal structures and make you feel, think and perceive in ways that are unnatural to a primordial human being. They trick your body into secreting hormones in amounts that should never be excreted by overstimulating you with simulacra of real experiences. Like a drug user, your body needs to be detoxified from this.

The next easiest aspect to tackle is changing your diet. Read the ingredients lists of the foods you buy at the supermarket. If you cannot pronounce some of the words in that list or do not know what they are – do not buy it. Simple. Avoid added sugars, preservatives, genetically modified foods, processed foods, soy (especially if you are male) and an overindulgence of caffeine. And obviously consume ample amounts of fresh fruits, vegetables and water. Whatever you like to eat, find clean, natural, organic, healthsome versions of those foods if you can afford it. If you cannot afford it, do your best. The chemicals in our foods, and even the foods themselves, are among the things which shape our thoughts and feelings without us realizing it. There are heavy metals put in our foods but in such small amounts that the Food and Drug Administration does not require that food corporations write them on the ingredients lists. The link between aluminum and Alzheimer's disease was discovered not too long ago, and we have long known of the link between mercury and a plethora of mental disorders, and now we are being tricked into consuming titanium as well when titanium dioxide is put into milk and rice in order to make them appear more white and therefore allegedly more appealing and marketable.

If the food is produced by some brand name major corporation, it is best not to eat it. And be wary of off brand companies as well and check to see if they are in fact owned by one of these major corporations. The competition in the food industry is largely an illusion these days as large corporate agribusiness entities are in complete violation of anti-trust laws which seem to be going unenforced. These groups are seeking a monopoly on the food supply and we have seen throughout history that nothing good ever comes from that. They clearly have a desire to force us to eat things which are just awful for our bodies and minds. The path of genetic modification and chemical alteration of the food supply is not some saving grace to end world hunger as naive college students and science degree holders have been tricked into proselytizing. Agribusiness has been putting synthetic fertilizers, chemicals, and genetic modifications in our food since the 1980's and food prices have only increased along with levels of hunger and malnutrition and our soil quality has been plummeting. Judge the tree by its poisoned fruits and cast away the lies coming from the media, the government, the corporations and "scientific" researchers.

***

Aside from food, the type of mathematics we study and utilize also has an effect on our minds. Some of humanity's cognitive development can be charted by noticing the development from Euclidean geometry to the geometric systems of Gauss and Riemann and the extra step forward which was taken by James Clerk Maxwell.

When perception is dominated by the two dimensions of length and width, Euclidean geometry is used. But when the third dimension of depth dominates perception, Euclidean geometry breaks down and becomes unusable. Two parallel lines when seen close up appear obviously parallel, but when they extend outward away from the perceiver, they appear to meet at the horizon and are therefore not parallel from this perspective. Gauss and Riemann developed geometries that deal with this perceptual shift, and James Clerk Maxwell developed mathematics that dealt with dimensions higher than the third. As human imagination and cognitive powers developed to deal with more dimensions, our mathematics developed right alongside.

However, there was backlash within the halls of academia against the adoption of non-Euclidean mathematics, especially against James Clerk Maxwell. When Maxwell's first published math textbook was released, a man by the name of Dr. Heaviside was outraged by the higher dimensional mathematics and considered them charlatanry and heresy. Dealing with fourth, fifth and sixth dimensions seemed ludicrous, and using his power as a scholastic textbook editor, he deleted all of Maxwell's higher dimension mathematics from the second edition and left in only the two and three dimensional information. It seems he wanted to keep college students on the heavy side of life down here in the third dimension. (Sometimes I wonder if names like these are even real or some type of pseudonym or synchronicity.)

Riemann and Gauss were also harangued by mathematicians and architects. There was a great deal of resistance against putting these geometric systems to use especially in scholastic settings. But fortunately for us, the vast majority of the human race up to that point had no interest and very little education in mathematics, Euclidean or otherwise, and so the only resistance against Gauss and Riemann came from a relatively small number of stuffy academics who were jealously attached to their old dogma and the new novel geometric systems won the day and were eventually adopted and put into use.

But imagine if everyone in the world had been exposed to Euclidean geometry constantly, every day since the days of Euclid roughly two thousand five hundred years ago – not just the architects and geometers. Imagine if all human minds in this world were deeply entrained and conditioned with constant reinforcement of Euclidean mathematics through artificial means, maybe through text book reading and education, theatrical performances, religious rites, or through any other everyday occurrences and activities. One could imagine that by the time Riemann, Gauss and Maxwell came around, there might have been a great deal more resistance against their new and novel ideas. Instead of a handful of stuffed-shirts, now they would be contending with popular opinion on a large scale. It is even possible that we might not be accustomed to three-dimensional imagination if we had been entrained enough and most people would not see the purpose or benefit of Gaussian/Riemannian geometry. Perhaps our cognitive development would have been stifled to the extreme and minds like Gauss, Riemann and Maxwell would not have even been born.

This makes me wonder about the new and increasingly popular technologies of augmented reality and virtual reality. These things are rapidly growing in sophistication and affordability. They use a combination of Euclidean and Gaussian geometry and modern digitally-driven data science to overlay information on a two-dimensional screen atop a real-time image of the physical world (in the case of augmented reality) and to create artificial digital worlds from scratch juxtaposed against and instead of the real world (in the case of virtual reality.)

These technologies are being marketed and sold not only as novel entertainment, but as eminently practical cognitive enhancements to be used daily in the fields of science, engineering, medicine, business, politics, art, archaeology, and education. There are increasing numbers of people being entrained by Euclidean and Gaussian/Riemannian geometry and modern data science. These digital representations juxtaposed and overlaid in front of the real world are right in front of their eyeballs and rigidifying their minds to the current cognitive model. Imagine the stagnating effect that this constant reinforcement may have on the minds of these people.

There are studies that have shown prolonged exposure to virtual reality causes myopia, dizziness, loss of balance, vergence-accommodation conflict, motion sickness, headache, the shutting down of up to half of the brain's neurons during use[37], increases in harmful rumination and violent emotions in gamers using headsets compared to gamers playing the same game without a headset on a computer who had no measurable increase in same[38], and temporary lack of depth perception and loss of spatial awareness after use[39]. The symptoms of this phenomenon have even been given a name: cybersickness[40].

I have used virtual reality multiple times in various settings and have experienced a handful of the symptoms listed above each time including nausea, headache, and a temporary loss of balance. I will not be using this technology ever again.

My concern is that this technology will

prevent the natural cognitive development toward higher dimensional perception and mathematics. Down the road in the future, when a brilliant new geometer is capable of perceiving the shortcomings of Gaussian/Riemannian geometry, or a brilliant cognitive scientist questions the dogma of data science, and they offer some new development, there may be far more resistance to these new ideas from an entrained public who have been conditioned by overuse of augmented and virtual reality systems. These technologies may trap our consciousness in the third dimension.

Imagine a butterfly that was incapable of breaking out of its cocoon.

Devices such as these, in my opinion, are Ahrimanic; they drag people into the Eighth Sphere, a place of stultification and materialism, of limitations in consciousness and feeling. Humanity may become solidified and crystallized at its current state and develop no further – perhaps even slip downward. These devices will perceive for you, they will use your eyes for you, they will think for you, they will imagine for you. No longer will you need to extend your inner and outer eyes to the horizon to contemplate what may be there – a machine will do that for you. Our imaginations, cognitive abilities, and spiritual faculties may atrophy.

***

Taking sovereignty over your mind and taking sovereignty over your body are the same thing. They go hand-in-hand and work in tandem. While you may have freedom of the mind without freedom of the body, you cannot have freedom of the body without freedom of the mind, but one of the first stages of purifying your mind is to purify your body. The Vajrasattva Buddhists call this purifying the body-mind and the mind-body. It is a reciprocal process where the distinction between mind and body becomes less pronounced and their unity enhanced.

The Electronic Doppelgänger

There is a misconception held commonly by marketing corporations, data scientists, and pop psychologists that an accurate psychological profile can be built by data-mining a person's internet history and social media activity. The only profile that they will discover is the distorted image of that person's electronic doppelgänger. This is why law enforcement investigators will still follow their targets around the old fashioned way for weeks or months with cameras and binoculars because they have realized that data-mining does not work correctly in the real world. It may work somewhat in limited instances to advertise something to you that you may wish to purchase, but beyond that, it actually tells them next to nothing about a person aside from the most basic characteristics that are generally not unique to that person or signify very much about their motivations or future actions, and anomalous data that appears may be taken far too seriously or in some cases, not seriously enough. Psychological profile building is far more complex and unreliable than most people realize.

On the average, almost everyone's internet history is the same. People shop for basic necessities and luxury items, they search for tutorials and instructions in arts and practical disciplines, they watch porn, they send and receive messages for work and social life, they attempt creative pursuits, they play games, they satisfy their morbid curiosities (you might be surprised by the number of totally normal people who search how to build bombs or how to stop blood-flow to the brain. Despite what you may think, it actually does not indicate that they wish to harm anyone. They may simply be bored or researching something specific.) They use social media to promote their small businesses or to appear happier and more successful than they actually are, and they desperately attempt to fill the void of loneliness, emptiness and sadness that they feel which is caused by our meaningless and pedantic culture.

You won't learn much more than that about a person by data-mining their internet activity. Every old school investigator knows that if you wish to know a person, you must see them in real life living out their day. You must watch them sit on a park bench and feed the winged rats. You need to see them standing on their front porch staring into the sky. You have to observe them opening doors and holding them open for someone else walking through or allowing it to close in their face. You need to watch them interact with strangers and see their minor facial expressions and body language. You must hear their voices when encountering a frustrating experience that comes out of the blue. You must observe them as they dance to their favorite music alone in their living room. You must also poke and prod them and confront them. There is far too much about a person to observe that is necessary for building an accurate psychological profile and even the most adept investigators and psychologists know that they will come up short even after months and months of spying. Many people lack the empathy and intuition to accurately understand a person. An increase in data collection does not translate as an increase in understanding, and a lack of data does not necessarily result in a lack of understanding. Psychological profiles are still considered hackneyed nonsense in many areas of law enforcement and are always taken with a gigantic grain of salt. So when pop psychologists, marketers, bloggers and internet influencers tell you that these tech corporations know more about you than you know about yourself, unless you completely lack self-awareness, it is utter nonsense, a sensationalistic sound byte. They may think they know. They may wish to know. They may spy on you twenty four/seven through your phone's camera and microphone, through CCTV cameras all over town, and through your internet router. They may keep track of your biometric data through "health" apps, but they will never truly know you. All they see is an electronic signal of you: sound, video, text and digital data. It is not you they are perceiving, but your doppelgänger.

This digital double that people have created of themselves which is stored in servers all over the world in a virtual realm is akin to the occult concept of the Guardian of the Threshold. This entity is an amalgamation of all your deep, dark urges, thoughts, beliefs, regrets, actions, desires, hopes and fears. It is a psychic creature composed of all the worst, most perverted, sad, pathetic and evil things of which you are capable. And you must face this creature as one of your final trials before entering the higher worlds of Spirit and enlightenment. It is a distorted yet true reflection of yourself which guards the Abyss, the infinite gulf, which you must cross between your human self and your suprahuman destiny. If you utilize computer technology, the internet and social media as a standard part of your life, you are allowing this entity to have more power, to actually begin to enter into the physical world itself and take shape within the digital realm. The more you use these technologies in a mindless and unconscious way, the more you allow the reflection of this entity to give birth to itself.

At this point, you may not only need to face this entity during your spiritual initiation before crossing the Abyss to enlightenment, but you may need to face it on this plane when the Pre-Crime Thought Police arrest you because they suspect you are about to murder someone based on your internet history, or when your paranoid girlfriend imagines you are cheating on her because there was a bikini-clad girl in one of your selfies, or when your father kicks you out of the house because you posted slutty pictures of yourself on social media for everyone to see, or when the government increases your taxes because they noticed you made an online purchase of a new row boat, or when your wife divorces you because she saw you ordered a sex doll, or when the local religious council revokes your priesthood status because they saw you subscribe to Tarot reading videos, or when your Tarot reading book club revokes your membership because they saw that you subscribe to Christian preachers on the same website, or when your parole officer kicks in your front door and sends you back to jail because he saw you purchased plane tickets which were in reality a gift for your sister.

As you can surely imagine, data-mining your doppelgänger has the potential to ruin your life especially if you lack the ability to control your urges or if your innocent activity is misconstrued as deviant or malevolent by intolerant and ignorant people. Instead of facing your Guardian of the Threshold at the proper time of your spiritual maturity, a digital reflection of it will face you at an unfortunate time and potentially derail your entire life. But perhaps people need this to happen. Perhaps it is simply a rude awakening which would force people to face themselves who otherwise would not. Who am I to say? All I know is that if you are aware of this issue, you may rise above it through self-awareness, self-control, temperance and spiritual discipline. It is my recommendation that you do not give virtual life to this psychic creature by unconsciously using your computer and phone. Be totally aware and in complete remembrance of yourself when utilizing these technologies. Think very carefully about all of your internet activity and do your best to prevent lapses in judgment.

***

Acquiring spiritual concepts throughout our lives can be very uncomfortable. Most people prefer what is tangible, something they can hold, something they can feel in their hands or something of which they can take a photograph. These things are easy to grasp, easy to understand, easy to experience and utilize. It is much easier to buy a soft mattress and lie down on it than it is to know what happens to you after your body dies. It is much easier to grab a handful of chocolates and stuff your face with them than it is to contemplate how spiritual entities live within each other and within us and how to make the most of these connections. It is much easier to lose oneself in material comforts and distractions than it is to learn of spiritual things. No one pays you to learn about these things. No sense gratification results from learning about these things. Yet if you do not take the time and effort to learn of these things in this life, you will be lost after your death. You will experience confusion and waywardness and either be drawn back by your worldly attachments to another incarnation that is relatively similar to the one you just experienced or be dissolved utterly in the primordial spiritual strata of reality. In short, your spiritual progress will have been very much lacking in this life.

In the past, it was much easier for people to acquire spiritual concepts due to the lack of material distractions available to them and the general inability to indulge in temptations. Today in this age of technology and instant gratification, there are so many distractions, conveniences, comforts, and temptations that it is much more difficult to acquire wisdom. In the past, people were much more capable of receiving a beatific vision or a spiritual insight simply by living a normal healthy life. There were far more spontaneous awakenings in, say, the medieval era than there are today. In today's world, most people who experience a beatific vision or a deep spiritual insight are those who have experienced a deprivation of something to which they were accustomed, and therefore; the awakening is not spontaneous, but induced as a psychic emergency measure.

We often hear of those who have had near

death experiences and the spiritual, inspirational and novel knowledge with which these people return. Only after they were nearly deprived of their life did they learn to appreciate it. We also hear stories of the rich person who lived the high life but then lost everything and in their poverty and lack, were forced to turn to their own inner resources and found the font of spiritual wisdom within. Or the rich person who became disillusioned with their wealth and luxury and had a catastrophic realization that there must be more to life. Only after they were deprived of their satisfaction with material wealth did they turn toward the spirit. Let us not forget the incarcerated man who once had a comfortable life of money, soft recliners, a distracting television set, sexual selection, and so on, but after being sent to prison, he lost all of that and is now locked in a tiny room with nothing to take his attention. He is forced to look within himself and discover his internal freedom. We also have victims of abuse and neglect who become spiritually active because they had to learn to rely on themselves and their internal strength in order to survive the horrible conditions that they have suffered. On the average, people in today's world tend to only turn toward spirituality after they have been disappointed or bored by this life or deprived of some comfort, distraction, opportunity or health.

It is extraordinarily rare today that

someone chooses the spiritual path when they are young, fit, healthy, and have potentially long futures full of opportunities. And I am very skeptical of those who do choose it at a young age. I have been around these people since my teenage years and many of them seem to want something. They practice hatha yoga because it helps them feel healthy and "de-stressed" from their work week – which is excellent and people should do this – however, it becomes deceitful when they pretend to have higher spiritual aspirations when in fact they do not. They practice yoga, meditation and other disciplines because it makes them appear spiritually mature and more attractive to potential sex partners. They read and quote scripture and other spiritually oriented literature because it makes them appear wise and gives them advantage over the gullible. Eventually when they reach their late twenties or thirties, they will abandon the spiritual path and focus on mundane goals and sense-enjoyments because there is a time limit to how long a person can keep up a disingenuous charade especially if they have not received the attention or gratification that they expected. The ones who do receive the gratification they expected and stick to this charade generally become malicious cult leaders or grifters of some kind. The world has no shortage of these types of personalities.

Perhaps you think I am being too critical,

that we criticize in others that which we hate about ourselves. This can be true at times, however; this is a book about the age of deception in which we live and we must not overlook fraudulence or delusion within the spiritual community. There were very good reasons that the ancient schools barred entry to the disingenuous and intellectually unfit. With the democratization of spirituality, we may indeed have an increase in the number of people who can achieve spiritual well-being, but we also have a commensurate increase in the number of opportunists, liars, charlatans and the lukewarm, halfhearted, confused and deluded. And these people are currently generating a great deal of data about themselves on the internet.

The true, unadulterated calling for a dedicated spiritual life in the heart of a young and healthy person who has not experienced deprivations is extremely rare and is generally found only in households and families full of love, balance and support which allow a child to blossom properly in early youth. These households will generally have a lack of technological distractions and the children will very likely be home-schooled or the child will have had the disposition and fortitude to resist the brainwashing that occurs in the schooling system. For a long time, these types of households have been diminishing in number and a few generations of people have matured in an almost entirely detrimental fashion, but thankfully due to the recent and increasing deprivations and hostilities of our own national and local governments and corporations against us, people are realizing the importance of these types of family structures and are currently reestablishing them. (Again, people tend only to turn toward the truly great and spiritual once they have experienced loss, frustration, deprivation or immanent threat of deprivation.)

This is where the electronic doppelgänger will have an enormous impact in the not-too-distant future on a great number of people. Today, our doppelgänger is used to advertise to us offers, enticements and temptations. But we do not see our doppelgänger being used in this way; we simply see the advertisements that result from its use. We are guided down the garden path of search results, video recommendations, social media content curation, music playlist recommendations, and even the headlines in our news feeds appear in a priority order that is dictated by the data which has been collected on us. Why are you being shown news articles about a war in Eastern Europe and someone else on the same news feed is being shown an article about a corn silo that burned down while a third person is being given an article about a new lipstick manufacturer?

If you could take all the data that has been

collected on you and see how marketers, media groups, governments and technology corporations compile and collate this data and how they use it to manipulate your emotions and thoughts, to get you to buy something, to vote for someone, to believe something, to yell at someone, to get angry about something, to become saddened by something, to be sexually aroused by something, to desire something you were not even thinking about, and the plethora of other underhanded and diabolical social engineering tactics employed to mold you and shape you and evoke specific behaviors from you so that they may dominate you, you would witness a grotesque monster, a perverted and terrifying reflection of yourself. You would see the weakest and most repugnant aspects of yourself magnified a thousandfold in the shape of a repulsive beastly caricature. You would in fact be witnessing a digital version of your Guardian of the Threshold.

    Witnessing this horrific distortion of yourself may evoke feelings of shame, guilt, and self-loathing as you stare into a mirror from a nightmare. All of your narcissistic social media posts, angry outbursts, toxic comments, perverted porn searches, lies and deceits, pointless consumeristic purchases, and desperate pleas for validation will be staring right back at you in a grotesque blob of undulating and oozing data alongside the ways in which this data has been used by nefarious groups to manipulate you. You will be witness to the indulgence of your own hedonism and the parts of yourself which were gullible, suggestible and easy to manipulate.

But honestly, as counter-intuitive as it may seem, the healthy reaction is to simply accept it as part of yourself and laugh at it and let it go. I used this negative language to evoke feelings of anxiety and acute self-awareness within you, to make you feel judged. It was a dirty trick. I am not judging you. You should check out my browser history. Promise yourself to do better, take the steps necessary and don't sweat it.

This can be an excellent opportunity to train yourself for the stage of spiritual development when you must face your Guardian of the Threshold and move beyond into higher worlds. It can be seen as a sparring match before the actual battle. It is the deprivation unto the point of depravity which forces non-spiritual people to adopt the path of spirituality, or for spiritually active people to gain in strength and determination – a recommitting to the path. As horrible as this time period may be, I have said it before in this book, it is a wonderful chance to do seriously effective spiritual work in a very short period of time. Every crisis is an opportunity. Every hardship and moment of harsh self-awareness comes with a chance to awaken your inner spirit. Ahriman (Satan to the Christians) was given a task by God to force humans to face themselves. We should be grateful to him for a job well done. After a few generations of facing our digital doubles in such a harsh way, I believe we will be much more likely to reestablish healthy family units and be much more conscious about how we raise future generations.

Fearing Death is The Best Way to Ruin Your Life

The single most detrimental attitude for a person's well-being is the fear of death. There is no single thing more capable of derailing, ruining, and misleading a person's life than being afraid of this inevitable and natural phenomenon. It is the most potent tool that expert manipulators use to gain power over other people. They will exploit and play upon a person's fear of death to get them to do whatever they want. It is also the one thing that people use against themselves in order to justify cowardice, mediocrity and complacency.

In an anti-spiritual world such as the one in which we live, fear of death is the engine of almost everything. It is the impetus of government, it is the engine that drives the economy, it is the source of greed and consumerism, it is the cause of preemptive military actions, it alters how people engage with their friends and family, it affects which type of career a person chooses, which spouse they select, it governs how much time they spend consuming entertainments and luxuries, it determines what types of risks they are willing or unwilling to take, whether or not they will stand up for someone else or even for themselves, it will inform what they believe in or want to believe in, what they say or want to say, it will determine how obedient a person is to a tyrant, in short, it will affect nearly every decision a person makes and every desire or aversion a person feels. This is why we must not fear death. To fear it is to be ruled by the fear of it. Death comes for us all. It happens to every single one of us. It is going to happen to you one way or another. You might as well get on board with this idea now instead of fighting this reality unto your final breath. Do you want to go out kicking and screaming in fear, confusion and denial, or would you rather meet your end with serenity, dignity, and honor?

Those who fear death are prime candidates for citizenship in the dystopian technocracy which is coming down the pike (a.k.a. The Eighth Sphere.) The technocracy that is taking shape before our very eyes, the technocracy which is taking advantage of the rotting corpse of Western Civilization in which we live, is preying upon people's insecurities and delusions about life and death. People are encouraged to take into their bodies the toxic and harmful products of pharmaceutical corporations from a fear of dying. People are encouraged to act like promiscuous, narcissistic, greedy degenerates because they are inculcated with the "You Only Live Once" mentality of fulfilling every hedonistic desire you can before you hit your expiration date. To hell with the consequences. Governments easily whip people up into a warlike frenzy by claiming that their way of life is under threat and will die. God forbid the Great and Holy Ideology of Democracy should ever be transgressed! We must kill to protect it from being killed! Slaves would rather remain slaves than to risk being killed in a rebellion. Would-be patriots remain lazy couch potatoes and hot-air hypocrites because they would rather not risk their salaried income and comfortable home by standing up and fighting against their oppressive shadow government. The fear of death is the main reason why our world is in such a dark age at the moment. To change this age would require a great deal of sacrifice which so few are willing to make.

It is only a matter of time before technology corporations begin to offer immortality through technical, pharmaceutical, or genetic means. Such companies are already working on ways to upload human minds into virtual worlds and allowing their bodies to fall into a perpetual medically-induced vegetative state which they consider to be a realistically attainable vision of heaven. Others are working on ways to genetically or mechanically augment human bodies to increase their lifespans indefinitely and finally "curing the disease of death." This is the same method that religious institutions have used to subdue entire populations to their will. They promise a cure for death. They claim the keys to the kingdom of life everlasting. Transhumanism and technocratic modalities are simply the atheist's religion. So long as you fear death, you are easy prey for corporations, governments, cults and religious institutions. You are at risk of becoming a member of the flock of a new religion or subject of a tyrannical government regime.

This new technocracy being foisted upon us relatively unawares will be a blending of government, corporate business, medicine, political activism, and religion. These institutions will merge into a super-state, a meta-culture fueled by religious fervor, fanaticism and intolerance. Those with eyes are aware of these developments and there is a real resistance against them. It is imperative that this resistance continues to grow in strength and determination.

When one civilization collapses, two civilizations tend to begin to grow in its stead: one better than the previous civilization and one worse. The worse one is born of our lower animal impulses and the conspiracies of those opportunists who are hungry for power. The better one is built on the human spirit which strives toward wholeness (holiness), transcendence of the mundane, and the integration of the mundane and the spiritual. Animals and conspirators fear death. It is why they act the way they do – to preserve their life, their power and their wealth for as long as possible. Humans do not fear death. It is why they are able to create great cultures based upon spirit, love, heroism, order and light – things which require great sacrifice of life and wealth.

The problem with the resistance against the bad type of civilization being built is that most of these well-meaning resistors are lost in the old Western Civilization. They dream of days gone by and are attempting to restore them. They see tradition when they should instead be seeing The Tradition. They believe that there was some ideal time when things worked better, and in many instances they are absolutely correct. But what is past is past. It cannot come back. These types fear that the West is dying or has already died and they do not wish to let it go. They want to resuscitate it, to put it on life support, and dwell with it in its cold and sad hospital room reminiscing about the good old days until they both finally expire of old age. I have sympathy, but absolutely no patience, for these types of conservatives. They are conservatives only to the extent that they wish to "conserve" an earlier form of something they prefer. They do not wish to conserve The Tradition. Most of them do not even know what The Tradition is. If they heard this phrase, they would think: Catholic Tradition, Jewish Tradition, Pagan Tradition, the 1950's Traditional Man and Traditional Woman, Constitutional Tradition, Patriotic Tradition, etc.

They would not realize that The Tradition refers to that which gives rise to the human spirit itself. That Law which governs all of Reality is The Tradition – it is not some institution or some bygone set of cultural customs or values. It is not some slice of history that one can point to and say, "Hey! That's the Tradition!" It is the very Spirit of the Cosmos. It is the Absolute Cause of All Causes, the Unconditioned, the Beginningless and Endless, the Unborn and Undying. Nothing can be before It, after It, inside It, outside It, older than it, or beyond It. It can neither be nor not be. It can neither become nor not become. It is the Absolute Origin, Home and Destination of All that Is. It is Unknowable, Unthinkable. It Is.

This is what must be conserved in our world. This is what must be the very foundation and heart of our next civilization. The West is dead. Do not deny or fear this. All organisms die. It is time to build and be born anew. The Tradition is the only cause and creator of great civilizations and Its civilizations always become old and corrupted and will die eventually, like trees in the forest. It does not matter. What happens to the future of our new civilization is not important. We leave that in the hands of those spirits and humans in whose hands it shall fall. All that we can do now is thank and honor the West for having existed, thank and honor our ancestors for doing all they have done, let it all go, and connect to the Source of All Reality and give It a home in our hearts. Honor your ancestors by acting with courage, heroism and creativity – not by lamenting the fact that they are dead. When we do this, all of our actions will be dedicated to The Tradition and we shall begin to build a great civilization with It as the foundation and the purpose. We build our civilization from The Above and oriented toward The Above. We cannot know exactly what It wants from us, but when we honor It and allow It space to develop Its Divine Will within our lives and through us into the world, we can rest assured that our decisions and actions will be used by It to generate a society worthy of our children.

It is the hub of the wheel. Anything that turns and spins on the spokes or the rim is not Traditional. Anything subject to change, decay, and death is not Traditional. Although that which The Tradition creates is subject to change, decay, and death, It Itself is not. Identify this hub, sit in the center with It, allow all the phantasmagoria of life in this world, of the rise and fall of civilizations and institutions, to pass before you like leaves on a river or like a movie screen. Do not attach yourself to any particular culture or society or idea. Attach yourself to the hub of the wheel, center yourself in It and feel the stillness. No longer will you rise and fall with civilizations or political and cultural trends. No longer will you be swept up by your emotions or desires. You will be as immovable as It.

From this center, you will be an instrument of It. To the extent to which you have adhered to It, It will use you to build a new world in accord with all that is just and righteous. To the extent to which you still fear the death of something, some value, some custom, some tradition, even yourself, you are not in the center. You might not even notice that you are being used in such a way. Your actions and decisions will simply be in alignment with the creation of a better culture. Your choices, your words, your deeds will be like seeds planted in the hearts and minds of those around you which will grow and blossom in their own time and in their own way. The Divine will nurture the seeds you plant.

In order to achieve this alignment, this freedom from the fear of death, you must face your own death. There are severely practical instructions for this in the Japanese Samurai tradition codified in two books known as *Bushido* and *Hagakure*. I highly recommend reading them. In short, imagining your death as often as possible and in as many ways as possible is the best way to prepare for the eventuality. Imagine your body being torn apart by dogs or cut apart by a sword. Imagine being run through the heart or shot in the head. Imagine getting cancer and dying of this disease. Imagine getting flattened by a Mack truck or burned in a building fire. Simply imagine getting old and drifting away in your sleep. If this makes you nervous or squeamish, then all the more reason to do it with determination and courage. Do it until it no longer makes you feel nervous or squeamish. Then one day, should you find yourself in a fearful situation such as being mugged at gunpoint or hitting a pocket of turbulent air during airplane travel, you may find that you are serene and that you really do not care whether or not you die in this moment. It is then that you will know you have achieved freedom from the fear of death. It is then that you will know from now on you are capable of heroic action.

If you can overcome the fear of your own death, how much easier it is to overcome the fear of the death of your civilization – how much easier it is for you to carry out the heroic deeds necessary to build a new and better one.

But it does not end there. Freedom from the fear of death and the ability to carry out heroic deeds is half the battle. The other half is resisting the lures and temptations of joining with the worse civilization being constructed. Nihilism, hedonism, atheism, materialism, consumerism, transhumanism, money, and complacency will all act as enticements which will attempt to derail your spiritual path and have you fall into the trap of living within the technocracy and giving your lifeforce to it.

Again, I would like to emphasize that I am not a Luddite. Utilizing technology is not the same thing as having a culture and civilization based on technology (a.k.a. technocracy.) Society should be based upon the Absolute Source of Reality, God, Tao, The Law, That Which Is. If your culture is based upon That and firmly rooted in It, then whatever technologies you develop will be in harmony with Divinity and can more-or-less be utilized freely. If your culture is instead based on technology itself or based upon scientific theories or utilitarian desires, there are an infinite number of paths that can lead to confusion and self-destruction for there is no guarantee as to the effects these technologies based on theories, opinions or personal desires will have on the health and harmony of the people and the world.

So now you must take this freedom from the fear of death and use it as the foundation to find your freedom from the fear of suffering. They are much the same thing, at least they are based on the same fear. If you can stand firm, brave and serene in the face of death, you must extend that capability and become firm, brave and serene in the face of that which causes death such as illness, age, bodily harm, poverty, deprivation and so on. It is not much of a leap – it is not a very big step to take. Again, just imagine it as often as you can. When you are no longer afraid of the things which cause death, then you can extend this capability yet further and make yourself free from the fear of general suffering, even the suffering that does not cause death. There is only one hang up: death is easy. Suffering that leads to death is also easy because we are assured it ends with its own cessation in death. Suffering in general is difficult when there is no promise of it ending soon.

This type of suffering, the mild or non-fatal type of suffering that has the potential to go on and on for prolonged periods of time is what causes true terror in many people. Chronic loneliness, chronic illness, chronic pain, chronic anything can be paralyzing. This is the essential fear that keeps people in line, keeps them obeying the law, keeps them going to work and collecting money, keeps them in horrible jobs, keeps them buying things, keeps them believing detrimental beliefs, keeps them in unhealthy relationships, keeps them living a life that is just good enough to keep prolonged suffering at bay. But is that life good enough to allow you to follow your true calling? I imagine it is not. Following a calling usually requires a great risk, a large gamble, a jumping into the unknown, and there is no promise of success. You may fail, you may be hurt physically or emotionally, you may be rejected, you may fall into poverty, you may even die. The fear of suffering has the capability to prevent you from living your best life. However, there is a distinct possibility if you can move beyond this fear: you may succeed. You may dive into the unknown and realize that there was nothing to fear after all. Or perhaps there will be much suffering for a time, but on the other end of that suffering is glory and joy having lived a life without regret or apprehension. You tried your best. You gave it your all. Trying and failing is better than not trying at all. Trying and failing gives you an immense spiritual reward at your time of death. You will feel self-satisfied having given it your best shot. Not trying leaves you feeling inadequate, ashamed and stupid on your death bed. Which would you prefer?

If you can achieve this freedom from the fear of suffering, you will be invincible in the face of all temptations and lures that would lead you astray. You will be incorruptible. You will accept no bribes, no false promises, no distractions of any kind. This is the type of freedom that makes you truly human and will enable you to be suprahuman. Remaining in possession of these fears will keep you in the animal kingdom and you will be treated like cattle.

The Only Way Out is Through

If you have made it through this book, you are a trooper. This meandering excursion through occult spiritual doctrine, paranormal research, reactionary conservatism, and Traditional revivalism certainly is not for everyone. I have spent my entire life since early childhood studying, exploring and synthesizing occult, spiritual, paranormal, scientific and historic ideas and what I have learned is that transcendent realities, however important they are for people to understand, are essentially impossible to describe adequately. All I can do is point in certain directions and offer practical tools to help you think about these things. I cannot tell you what to think, but I can help you figure out how to think.

I have found that the most financially successful and famous spiritual teachers are the ones who tell people what to think. They offer answers to questions so that the seekers who are vexed by such questions can forget about them, happy that they have learned the answer and ready to lay their heads down at night and fall asleep quickly without being plagued by uncertainty and ignorance. Answers are sexy. Answers are desirable. Answers grab people's attention. Answers get clicks. Answers get website traffic. Answers sell books. People are oh so grateful for answers. Answers provide a warm and fuzzy feeling of assurance. And more often than not, answers are wrong.

I cannot offer you answers. At least not very many. I would not insult your intelligence by attempting to convince you of something that I know you can figure out on your own. I am the kind of person who, when asked a question, generally answers it by asking a question to the questioner. You have the answer which you seek within yourself. Sometimes you may need some guidance, someone who can provide you with a nice set of tools, but you never need an answer from someone other than yourself.

The more one learns, if they are honest with themselves, the more they realize that they know nothing – the more they realize that really no one knows anything. However, we have an inner compass that tells us the quality of our decisions and actions. We can listen to this compass, we can ask it questions and wait for it to respond. Generally, this compass can be felt in the solar plexus. We can consider decisions we have made or wish to make and focus our attention on this spot within ourselves and wait for it to give us a pang of conscience, urging us to reconsider, or a feeling of bolstered fortitude letting us know that the correct, or mostly correct, course of action was taken or will be taken. Beyond this, not much knowledge is necessary to live a good life.

If reading this book has provided you with even just one tool or one moment of insight that will aide you in navigating this post-modern world in which we live, then I will have done my job. Everywhere I turn, I see people drowning – drowning in politics, drowning in technology, drowning in animalistic desires, drowning in greed, drowning in work, drowning in bad relationships, drowning in confusion, drowning in consumerism, drowning in lies and deceptions, drowning in false realities and false senses of self. This is to be expected when a wayward culture is in decline and their previous civilization is dead or dying. I hope that I have not only offered you the blueprints to build a lifeboat and get off of this sinking ship, but a map and compass which you can use to find safe harbor. I also hope that I have provided you with a shield to protect yourself from the assaults against the human spirit that come from all quarters.

I am not a doom and gloom kind of guy. I see multiple civilizations developing and growing in this world, some good and some not-so-good. I see a multi-polar future for humanity; a future where one civilization is unable to eradicate the others – a future of more choice of lifestyle. If you refuse to live in this burgeoning technocracy, learn a new language and find a new home. There are better places to live. If you do not wish to be guilty of grass-is-greener syndrome and you want to stay put, then you must be willing and ready to accept the troubles that lie ahead – the new government programs and policies, the new consumer technologies, the new agribusiness and food supply, the new social contracts, the new military protocols, and so on. You must know how to flow like water between and through them. You must know how to establish a better culture within and in spite of this one that is being built around you. You must be able to fight when necessary, retreat when necessary, speak out when necessary, and protect yourself from all the things which seek to diminish and enslave your soul.

We have a hard road ahead of ourselves and we may fail in the West. It is possible that our spirit will lie dormant and low for three thousand years or more because of these developments. We may not regain our spark for millennia. Look to the lands where once stood Great Pyramids and megalithic temple complexes. What has transpired there for the last few thousand years? Who has built structures of equal splendor? Who has developed spiritual traditions of equal magnificence? Where have those cultures gone? Such are the cycles of fortune and time. Such is very likely the fate of the West.

But I am no fortune teller. Nor am I a pessimist. I believe that anything is possible. I believe renewal and rejuvenation can be achieved at any point. The alchemy necessary to achieve this is rare and difficult, but not impossible. It usually requires an infusion from other cultures to remind us what truly matters after we have spent so many centuries with our heads up our own rear-ends. Look to the ascending civilizations, the cultures that have bright futures, and be honest with yourself about what needs to be done to improve our own.

Bibliography

1. Steiner, Rudolf. Lecture GA93a, Berlin, Germany, 9 October 1905. www.rsarchive.org

2. Ouspensky, P.D. (1949). *In Search of the Miraculous.* Harcourt, Inc.

3. Steiner, Rudolf. (2006). *The Evolution of Consciousness.* Rudolf Steiner Press.

4. Hesiod. Translated by Evelyn-White, Hugh G. (2018). *Theogony, Works and Days, and the Shield of Heracles.* Digireads.com Publishing

5. Translated by Wilson, Horace Hayman. (1840). *The Vishnu Purana.* John Murray, London.

6. Lao Tzu. Tranlated by Wu, John C.H. (1961). *Tao te Ching.* Shambala Publications, Inc.

7. Evola, Julius. Translated by Stucco, Guido. (1995). *Revolt Against the Modern World.* Inner Traditions International.

8. Yogananda, Paramhansa. (1946). *Autobiography of a Yogi.* Philosophical Library, Inc.

9. Steiner, Rudolf. Translated by Bamford, Christopher. (1994). *How to Know Higher Worlds.* Anthroposophic Press.

10. Keel, John A. (1975). *The Eighth Tower: On Ultraterrestrials and the Superspectrum.*

Saturday Review Press

11. Shakespeare, William. (1601). *Hamlet.* Nelson Doubleday, Inc.

12. Vallée, Jacques. (1979). *Messengers of Deception: UFO Contacts and Cults.* Daily Grail Publishing.

13. Moran, Mark and Sceurman, Mark. (June 15, 2020). *Aliens Came in Peace to High Bridge, NJ. https://weirdnj.com/stories/unexplained-phenomena/howard-menger-high-bridge/* Weird N.J.

14. Jung, Carl Gustav. (1959). *Flying Saucers: A Modern Myth of Things Seen in the Skies.* MJF Books.

15. Lippard, S. J.; Berg, J. M. (1994). *Principles of Bioinorganic Chemistry.* University Science Books.

16. Vallée, Jacques. (1969). *Passport to Magonia.* Daily Grail Publishing.

17. Holiday, F.W. (1990). *The Goblin Universe.* Xanadu Publications.

18. Ximénez, Francisco; Translated by Tedlock, Dennis. (1995). *Popol Vuh.* Simon & Schuster.

19. Collins, Andrew and Little, Gregory. (2022). *Origins of the Gods.* Bear & Company.

20. Beckley, Timothy Green. (1990). *Mystery of the Men in Black: The UFO Silencers.* Inner

Light Publications.

21. Corso, Philip J. and Birnes, William J. (1997). *The Day After Roswell.* Pocket Books.

22. Keel, John A. (1970). *Why UFOs: Operation Trojan Horse.* Manor Books, Inc.

23. Authorized New King James Version. *Holy Bible.* World Bible Publishers.

24. Hansen, George P. (2001). *The Trickster and the Paranormal.* Xlibris Corporation.

25. Turner, Victor W. (1969). *The Ritual Process: Structure and Anti-Structure.* Aldine de Gruyter.

26. Steiner, Rudolf. (1993). *The Fall of the Spirits of Darkness.* Rudolf Steiner Press.

27. Dugin, Alexander. (2012). *The Fourth Political Theory.* Arktos Media Ltd.

28. Rennie, John. (February 15, 2011). "The Immortal Ambitions of Ray Kurzweil: A Review of Transcendent Man." *Scientific American.*

29. Figley, Charles R. (2012). *The Encyclopedia of Trauma.* SAGE Publications.

30. Bostrom, Nick. (2014). *Superintelligence: Paths, Dangers, Strategies.* Oxford University Press.

31. https://www.cia.gov/readingroom/collection/stargate

32. Fuller, Thomas. (1642). *The Profane State.* Roger Daniel. Cambridge England.

33. Spengler, Oswald. (1926). *Decline of the West.* Alfred A. Knopf.

34. Vallée, Jacques. (1979). *Messengers of Deception: UFO Contacts and Cults.* Daily Grail Publishing.

35. Prokofieff, Sergei. (2009). *The East in the Light of the West.* Temple Lodge.

36. Government of the United States of America. (2023). "Drug Scheduling." https://www.dea.gov/drug-information/drug-scheduling

37. Gent, Edd. (2016). "Are Virtual Reality Headsets Safe for Children?" Scientific American. https://www.scientificamerican.com/article/are-virtual-reality-headsets-safe-for-children/.

38. Lavoie, R., Main, K., King, C. et al. *Virtual Experience, Real Consequences: The Potential Negative Emotional Consequences of Virtual Reality Gameplay.* Virtual Reality 25, 69–81 (2021). https://doi.org/10.1007/s10055-020-00440-y

39. Berger, Bennat. (2021). "The Psychological Implications of Virtual Reality." HackerNoon. https://hackernoon.com/the-psychological-implications-of-virtual-reality.

40. Government of the United Kingdom. (2020).

"The Safety of Domestic Virtual Reality Systems." https://assets.publishing.service.gov.uk/government/uploads/system/uploads/attachment_data/file/923616/safety-domestic-vr-systems.pdf.

www.ingramcontent.com/pod-product-compliance
Lightning Source LLC
LaVergne TN
LVHW010156070526
838199LV00062B/4381